SUPERCHARGE
YOUR EMOTIONS
TO WIN

SUPERCHARGE YOUR EMOTIONS
TO WIN

*7 Keys to Achieve
the Life You Desire
and Deserve*

BENJAMIN HALPERN

Genesis Book Publishing
BPS Books

Published in 2015 by
Genesis Publishing, an imprint of
BPS Books
Toronto and New York
www.bpsbooks.com
A division of Bastian Publishing Services Ltd.

ISBN 978-77236-008-0 (paperback)
ISBN 978-77236-009-7 (ePDF)
ISBN 978-77236-010-3 (ePUB)

Cataloguing-in-Publication Data available from Library
and Archives Canada.

Text design: Daniel Crack, Kinetics Design, www.kdbooks.ca

*To those who are, in essence, my co-authors:
the thousands of people who have allowed me
to be part of their transformation, in the process
teaching me the gift of the keys to manage
the supercomputer between my ears*

CONTENTS

KEY 4

Manage Your Emotions

KEY 5

Set and Attain Your Goals

KEY 6

Access the Power of Belief

KEY 7

Maintain Your Power

PREFACE

I am extremely pleased that a book has materialized from what for so many years has existed in my thoughts and practice. The efficacy of my approach to helping people win the life they desire and deserve has been proven by the thousands I have had the honor to serve directly through face-to-face counseling. But it has also been seconded by the many requests I receive daily in my offices for documentation of my approach. Now, *finally*, I can refer them to this book. After all, a book can travel to many people in many places a lot more quickly and effectively than one man with clients to counsel or seminars to conduct. And a lot less expensively, too!

Why is my approach successful? Because it helps people to access logic through what I call their emotional brain. Too many methods and books counsel change through logic and facts. But people aren't stupid. They get the reasoning behind change. They know that to lose weight you just have to eat less. And to get fit you just need to go to the gym daily. And to make money, you just need to make a lot of sales calls and follow through on the feedback you get until you hit the jackpot. However, as my book shows, the *limits* that people put on themselves to follow through on this kind of logic and knowledge must be dealt with first. And how is that done? By developing and attaching strong, productive emotions – *supercharged emotions* – to understanding and decision-making.

But who helped *me* to reach the outcome I desired – to publish this book? I would like to thank Theresa Dugwell, publisher of Genesis Publishing at BPS Books, for this and so much more. She was a recognized world champion as a runner before I met her, but through this project she became a champion for me on a personal level. When I shared my desire with her to reach a larger number of people with my seven keys, she picked up the baton and crossed the finish line, making my desire a reality.

Speaking of personal support, I would like to thank my dear parents, who have been there for me in every way possible from the moment I was born to this very day. May they continue in good health to reap the rewards of their hard work for many happy years to come. My thanks also to my siblings, who have been and continue to be an indescribably valuable source of support and inspiration that I can't imagine my life without.

Kudos to my dear children, who are G-d's most amazing and greatest gift. They make every day something to truly look forward to.

And last but not least, my heartfelt gratitude and deepest appreciation to my dear wife, because what I have achieved is all hers. She is my life partner. She has done more than her share in every way, and has created the perfect environment for me to thrive, and for that I am eternally indebted.

I look forward to meeting you, my readers, some day and hearing how you have supercharged your emotions to win.

BENJAMIN HALPERN, LCSW

INTRODUCTION

IF you felt unstoppable, would you approach a sales call differently? If you felt extremely confident, would you perform better in a business meeting? If you were in a very passionate state, would you make a better sales presentation? Chances are the answer to all these questions is a resounding YES!

Imagine that you just won a lottery. You would be extremely happy. But where would your lottery-winning feelings come from? If you've never won the lottery before, how would you know how to act and feel?

The answer is that many feelings are already in you, and have been from your youngest days. The challenge is to *access* the empowering and positive ones. Wouldn't it be useful if you could access them at will? To feel the supercharged emotions that are already inside you on a regular basis so you can win in your life?

When you're supercharged – when you live in an empowered emotional state – you can attain your dreams in every area of your life. You're then set up to win financially, mentally, emotionally, and spiritually – and in your relationships, too. Remember times in your life when you were just "on" and you just made things happen? Where did the supercharged emotions come from? From right inside you, of course!

And that is where this book comes in.

Supercharge Your Emotions teaches you the seven keys you must know to get the emotional leverage you need for success in every area of your life.

The keys are:

1 Clarify Your Outcome

2 Recognize What's in Your Control

3 Magnetize Your Thoughts and Actions

4 Manage Your Emotions

5 Set and Attain Your Goals

6 Access the Power of Belief

7 Maintain Your Power

KEY 1

CLARIFY YOUR OUTCOME

THE EMOTIONAL BRAIN

DOES it bother you that, despite your extensive knowledge of what you need to do and feel to win – gained from several books on the topic, online research, or even training sessions that you have attended – you still haven't reached the place where you want to be?

The answer is that logic and knowledge have very little to do with breaking through limitations. In fact, buying books and trying to understand the logic of what it takes to overcome your limitations and where you're going wrong is part of the problem. Your thinking patterns are a big reason that you don't get the outcomes you desire.

Logic has very little to do with bringing about change to your emotional brain. The emotional brain and the logical brain operate by two different sets of rules. Understanding and working with the logical brain won't give you control of the emotional part of your brain. When it comes to being able to master your limitations, it's the emotional part that you need to learn to manage.

Let me give you an analogy so you can appreciate and understand the difference between the two parts of your brain.

Think of road plates, those strong and solid sheets of metal, about five feet wide by ten feet long, that construction crews use to cover openings in the road. They are so strong, cars can drive over them safely.

Now, if I were to put one of them on a sidewalk, most people wouldn't hesitate to walk on it, because, safety-wise, it's the equivalent of a regular sidewalk. But what if I were to just change one variable? What if I placed the road plate outside the eightieth floor of the Empire State Building and across to the building on the other side of the street and asked you to walk across?

If you're like most people, you would balk at the very idea. If I were to ask you why, you most likely would say, "Because it's dangerous."

Let's say I then introduced logic to explain why it's totally safe, telling you, "This road plate was put in place by the same engineering team that built the famed Verrazano Bridge, and they have confirmed that it is equally as safe."

If I asked you whether you would stand on it now, what would you say? Chances are your answer would still be a resounding no.

You might say, "Maybe the weather's going to be windy."

I might respond by saying, "What if the entire team of meteorologists from radio station WCBS 880 vouched that the weather was totally fine and there wasn't going to be any wind? Would you walk on it then?"

"I'm not feeling well," you might say. "I couldn't possibly try it."

If I brought a team of doctors in to attest that you were perfectly healthy, would that do the trick? Not likely.

Logically, I showed you that walking on the plate eighty floors up is as safe as walking on it on the sidewalk below. But the reason logic has no sway over you is that you are accessing something a lot deeper than logic – your imagination.

You would look down at the road plate sticking out of the eightieth floor and down at the scene below, and ask, "What are those little rectangles moving around?"

And I would answer, "Those are buses."

"And what are those smaller rectangles?"

"Oh, those are cars."

"And what are those dots?"

"Oh, those are people."

And in your mind's eye – in your imagination – you would see a little red dot on the ground, and that would be you after you've fallen.

Logic goes out the window when imagination kicks in.

You could be assured a thousand times that you're going to be okay and it's totally safe, but you still wouldn't be able to bring yourself to do it. Because when you imagine something bad happening, all the logical explanations and assurances disappear.

This is why we get frustrated when someone tries to reason with us about doing something that scares us. Their logic doesn't help, because we can't get past our limiting thoughts. To get the results we want, therefore, we must alter our imagination. If we can do that, we can put a process of change in motion that will positively impact what we accomplish in life.

It Starts with Your Imagination

If you change your imagination	→ then →	*you change how you feel*
If you change how you feel	→ then →	*you change what you're going to do*
If you change what you're going to do	→ then →	*you change what you can accomplish*
If you change what you accomplish	→ then →	*you change your life*

IMAGINE THE GOOD

Controlling Your Imagination

Let's talk about how to take control of the part of your brain where imagination resides so you can use and control the creativity and sensitivity that G-d has given you.

After all, it is simply patterns of thought that have kept you stuck – *self-limiting patterns.*

If you were to interview ten thousand people with limitations, you would see that they share similar patterns of thought. And if you were to interview ten thousand people who live their dreams, you would see that they, too, share similar patterns of thought.

Imagine that two people are about to board an aircraft. One is nervous and the other calm. There's no biological difference between them other than what's happening in their brains. The nervous one is imagining that the plane is going to crash and he's about to meet his death. The calm person is imagining that he's arriving at his favorite vacation destination, excited about the great time he's going to have.

If we were to switch their thinking patterns, whereby the person who is calm is now imagining that he's going to die in an hour and the person who's nervous is imagining that he's going on his favorite vacation, their feelings would change.

It's all about imagination. If you imagine that something bad is going to happen and things aren't going to pan out the way you want, you're going to be stressed, despite any facts that your logical brain knows that may refute this.

Don't get me wrong. Logic serves a very powerful purpose. It keeps you in check so you don't imagine things that make no sense or are totally outside reality. You're not going to imagine walking through a street safely when there are cars coming at you at ninety miles an hour.

Yet you have the choice to always imagine that good things are going to happen, that things are going to pan out the way you want. If that's how you imagine things will be, that's how you're going to feel, regardless of what logic dictates.

The way people can walk on a tightrope, or over fire, is by using their imagination. Once they logically recognize that there's a way to do it safely *and they have the skill*, then all they need to do is imagine themselves on the other side safely.

That's right – success in a seemingly over-the-top endeavor is primarily about controlling your imagination.

Remember: When you control your imagination, you control your feelings. And when you control your feelings, you control the direction your life will take.

UNDERSTAND YOUR FOUR-PART BRAIN

Let me give you a model to help you understand your brain so you can make changes to your imagination and get started right away on getting what you really want.

The following model shows the four parts of your brain: the unconscious mind, the subconscious mind, the critical filter, and the conscious mind.

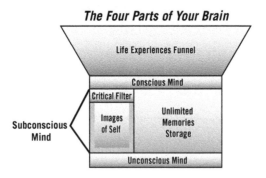

The Four Parts of Your Brain

Part 1 – Your Unconscious Mind

The job of the unconscious part of your brain is to control your heartbeat, your digestive system, your temperature, the blinking of your eyes, all the automatic processes. And it is under lock and key from G-d – and there's very little you can do to control that part of your experience.

Part 2 – Your Subconscious Mind

The subconscious mind is divided into two components.

Component A is the filing cabinet that stores every single memory you have ever experienced. According to researchers, we start storing information from the moment we're conceived. Even when we are in our mother's womb, we not only store information but can also access it. Some people believe that, through hypnosis, we can retrieve information from that time – that we can go back to our earliest experiences before and after birth and recall events. Even though we never experienced this time consciously, it was being recorded.

This component of the brain can store unlimited amounts of information.

Component B consists of our images of who we are and what we are. These are locked into our subconscious mind. They aren't easily accessible, and for good reason! If we were affected and changed by anything anyone ever told us about ourselves, life would be quite a roller-coaster ride for us. That's why these images are under lock and key.

Here's an example to help you understand this concept better. You see yourself as a healthy person with a healthy heart. Because this is locked into your subconscious mind, if you walk down the street and somebody tells you you're sick, it's not going to affect you. You *know* you're healthy.

Part of your job in achieving the life you desire is to make some changes to this part of your mind. But for now it suffices for you to know that this is part of your subconscious mind.

Part 3 – Your Conscious Mind

Your conscious mind is where you experience the thoughts you're aware of. The conscious mind is very limited! For example, scientists claim that it can hold only seven to nine bits of information at a time.

But it also serves a very important function. It is the doorway to the subconscious mind. Anything that your senses experience passes through your conscious mind on the way to your subconscious mind.

Part 4 – Your Critical Filter

If we experience something through our senses, why is it that we don't process *everything* consciously? Why are we not affected by *everything* we experience? The answer lies in the part of the brain called the critical filter, which is between your conscious mind and subconscious mind. It decides:

- which experiences will go in to the component of the subconscious mind that is just concerned with memory (it can be accessed at a later time without our even being aware that it was stored there), and

- which experiences in our conscious mind will reinforce those images we have of ourselves.

Going back to the example of your beliefs about your health, let's suppose we're friends and I tell you that your heart is weak. My statement would likely have no effect on you. It would go through your conscious mind and be funneled into the memory side of your subconscious mind. You're going to remember that I said it, but it's not going to affect the picture you have of yourself.

What would happen, though, if a cardiologist in a white coat made this statement to you? The information would go into the component of your subconscious mind that maintains the image of who you are, and it would affect that image. In no time at all you would see yourself as a person with a weak heart.

BYPASS THE CRITICAL FILTER

Let's understand how the critical filter works so you can see that you can sidestep it and create the changes you desire.

The critical filter refutes information based on old knowledge.

Children don't yet have a lot of information, so they have a very slight critical filter. They are easily affected by their parents' statements of what is right or wrong. Their impressionability can work for good or ill.

When parents tell children something about themselves – good or bad – they will accept it, because they don't have enough information to refute it. Children borrow their parents' critical filter in order to make judgment calls.

As children mature, their own critical filter becomes stronger and stronger. But certain things will still bypass it, such as information from an authority, as in my example above. That's one of the rules of the critical filter – that you don't refute an authority.

Let's say you have developed some negative views of yourself, of the world, or of certain situations, views that are now on the inside, having gotten past the critical filter. You now associate certain people, situations, yourself, and your life with these negative views. The connections between feelings and events are locked in and protected by your subconscious mind, on the other side of your critical filter, and your life runs accordingly.

By reading this book, you may have decided that it's time to go in and change these negative feelings. Your challenge is going to be to bypass the critical filter to see the changes that are needed and to make them.

Taking Control of Your Imagination

Again, the secret lies in your imagination.

The reason is simple. If you imagine something, and you can identify with it, you thereby utilize your conscious mind. To add the feelings you want to experience, you access the emotions that are locked away in your subconscious mind.

By attaching the feelings *that you choose to attach*, you can circumvent the critical filter. Over time, you can get good at this. You can start to slowly but surely change associations in your mind and give yourself feelings of calmness, security, safety, or confidence. Then you can begin to associate these feelings with various events and situations in your life as you see fit.

MAKE IT REAL

How Would You Like Your Life to Look?

Let's bring this discussion down to the practical level. As just discussed, the first part of creating emotional change is being able to imagine your desired outcome. If you can imagine something, you can slowly but surely begin to create the feelings to go with it. Attaching the feelings you want to attach requires you to bypass the critical filter. This is what will enable you to change the associations and the feelings connected in your subconscious mind. And by changing them, you change the way you feel and experience the world.

EXERCISE
Imagining How You Would Like Your Life to Look

List ten vivid images of situations you want to experience in which all your limitations have disappeared. As you envision a situation, also imagine the new, more positive feelings you want to associate with this new reality. Be clear on the emotions associated with each one. For example:

> I get up in the morning (situation)
> and
> I feel strong and confident (emotions).

All ten should be written and expressed in this way.

To help you get started, consider the following situations that many people say they would like to change.

- I speak in public and I feel…

- I am sitting at my desk and I feel…

- I talk to prospects and I feel…

- I get up in the morning and I feel…

- I am doing a sales presentation and I feel…

The entire exercise should take you five to ten minutes. The best way to do it is to spend somewhere between thirty to sixty seconds on each of these images, with your eyes closed. Studies show that when you close your eyes, it's much easier for your mind to create its imagery work. This approach will help you to successfully bypass the critical filter and see these associations taking root in your life.

1.

2.

3.

4.

5.

6.

7.

8.

9.

10.

Your goal is to be so clear about where you're heading that you can get past any obstacles that might block you from moving forward.

Working with Your Imagination and Brain

We all carry emotions that we're not aware of.

Someone might touch us on the shoulder the way someone touched us when we were sad, and all of a sudden we experience sadness. It has nothing to do with what we're doing; it's just an outside connection that was developed at one time.

Someone may look at us the way another person looked at us when we were feeling bad and – *boom* – we feel bad.

It's extremely important to be focused and know where you want to go in order not to be derailed by these obstacles.

When you're asleep at night, your critical filter relaxes. That's why you can dream about doing things that don't make logical sense. There's no filter saying, "That doesn't make any sense." By the same token, when you're awake, closing your eyes is a way you can tap in to that benefit and put the filter to sleep. It will strengthen your ability to imagine and heighten your ability to access your emotions.

If your goal is to wake up calm in the morning, then, before bedtime, spend thirty to sixty seconds imagining yourself getting up and being calm. Really juice your senses. See it as real, with color, sound, feeling, and smell. After thirty to sixty seconds of doing this, move on to your next picture until you have completed all ten.

At first, you may not see or feel things too clearly. With time, it will get better. This is how you start to take control of your imagination and your brain, and move in the direction you want to move.

As you proceed through the program, you're going to develop the skill and take control of the imagination part of your brain so you can access all the amazing feelings you already have within yourself on a day-to-day basis.

In my clinical work, when I initially ask people to do this, 99.9% formulate their intentions this way: I do x and I don't feel anxious.

That doesn't work. That's the equivalent of getting into the taxi and saying, "Don't take me here; don't take me there." This isn't language the brain can understand. You're not telling the brain where you *want* to go. It's like giving your brain the instruction, "Don't think of the color blue." We all know that will make us think of the color blue. We can't "not" think of something. What the brain interprets this to mean is to think of the color blue with an **X** over it.

That's not what you want. You don't want to feel anxious with an **X** sign over to it; you want to be calm and not anxious at all. So when you do this exercise, go over your list again. Be clear that you're saying where you *do* want to go, not where you don't want to go.

The brain is literal. It doesn't reinterpret. It doesn't change "I don't want to" into an understanding of what you *do* want. Clear and direct instructions are a language that your brain *does* understand.

I find that almost everyone can tell me what they *don't* want. It's not surprising for people to have been in therapy for years and still not know what they want; they simply have never thought about it.

It's important for you to know that you're never going to get beyond your limitations in that way. When people struggle to come up with an answer as to what the life of their dreams would look like, I say, "That's why you don't have it yet. You can't have something if you don't know what it looks like." It's as if they're standing in the street crying. I ask, "Why are you crying?" And they say, "Because I didn't get there yet." And I say, "Where?" And they say, "I don't know."

The Law of Attraction

In simple terms the Law of Attraction means you get what you think about, what you focus on, what you talk about, and what you believe. The question is: Is your balance of thought, communication, and belief more on the side of what you want or the side of what you don't want in your life?

Most people can articulate vividly and emotionally and in great detail all of the things that aren't going right in their lives. They are completely clear about who caused it and why they are so miserable and constantly tell anyone who will listen all about it. Do you know someone like this…perhaps you? Is it any wonder that they…or you…would continue to attract the same problems and situations over and over again?

Where your attention goes, energy flows!

What shows up in your life has less to do with where you were born, how you were raised, or what you look like than with what you focus on. Such factors do play a part in your expectations, but at any point along the way you can change your focus and stop using your past, your looks, and who you know as your excuse to not be living the life you really want for yourself.

If you want something to change, you have to change something!

KEY 2

RECOGNIZE WHAT'S IN YOUR CONTROL

CONTROL YOUR EMOTIONAL WORLD

God grant me the serenity to accept the things I cannot change;
the courage to change the things I can change;
and the wisdom to know the difference.
— Serenity Prayer

It is critical for you to recognize that you can't control everything. However, you do have control over what you need in order to create the life of your dreams.

When you focus on the part of life that is out of your control and try to change it and fail, then you feel like your life is out of your control. The emotions that stem from the feeling of being unable to control your experience and help yourself are anxiety, frustration, and depression.

On the other hand, when you focus on what you *can* control, you feel strong and empowered to move forward and attain your life's goals, aspirations, and dreams.

Here's an analogy to help you understand this better. Why do most people feel in control when they drive a car? Because they're focusing on the steering wheel, which is the part of the driving experience they fully control. Because, in essence they're mostly out of control when it comes to protecting themselves from getting killed in a car crash. Most accidents don't happen because a driver drives off the road but because another car crashes into their car.

When you focus on what's out of your control, you get

anxious, frustrated, and depressed. But when you focus on the part of life that you have the ability to control, you feel empowered and calm. When you focus on what's in your control, you feel empowered and have the internal drive to make things happen, because it's in your power to succeed.

One part of your experience that you *can* control is your emotions; you can make the rules as to when you experience a specific emotion. You also have the ability to turn emotions on or off. When you develop the skills to activate and deactivate your emotions, then you have the power to choose to supercharge your emotions so you win.

How Your Emotional Anchors Are Developed

You have millions of experiences in your lifetime. However, experiences do not in themselves have any emotions associated with them. Death is death. House is house. Car is car. Accident is accident. Child is child. Wedding is wedding. These are all neutral events and situations.

On the other hand, you have a vast range of feelings. We'll look at this in more detail later, but for now suffice it to say that there are many different feelings that you can apply to any experience.

According to developmental psychologists, by about age eight we've pretty much compiled in our subconscious mind all the different emotions we're going to experience in our life. These emotions become anchored to various events. There isn't any hardwired automatic connection between a specific event and specific emotion; it has to be developed.

Your life experiences play a major role in forming these connections; these experiences forge a connection between two unrelated entities. For example, there is no natural connection between being slapped and running onto a street. However, if a toddler runs into the street, he gets a smack from his parent for putting himself in grave danger. The toddler will connect street with smack and most likely not run onto the street again. If a child associates a lollipop with good behavior, she'll feel good when acting that way, even though, in essence, the behavior and the lollipop are two completely separate entities.

It is your mind that makes the connection between those two separate things. It's important to know that you have the ability to connect any feeling to any event.

This concept is going to prove very useful to you in freeing yourself from limitations and supercharging yourself to win. You have the ability to attach good emotions to desired actions and propel yourself towards your desired direction.

Your emotional world is like a compass – its needle always points north, which correlates to feeling good. You learn how to forge the connections between feeling good and your desired outcome. You learn to change and control your internal world so that the things that you choose to move towards are in line with your emotions. They can begin to move you in the proper direction and it feels good.

When you wind up in a problem situation, where for some reason something is causing you pain, fear, and stress, you can connect a different feeling or a different meaning to that situation. You have the choice to create a different feeling in response to any event that has caused you discomfort up to right now.

In essence you're not really changing a situation around you – and yet you are. *You're changing your whole world.* Because you're changing how you feel in a situation that in the past has been troublesome, you're freeing yourself from its clutches.

For example, suppose you have fear connected to heights. Remember that heights stay heights; this fact will never change. But you can change your feelings associated with heights. "Heights" doesn't specifically have to be connected with "fear." You can enable yourself to feel calm next to "heights," despite the fact that currently heights and fear are connected.

Why? Because experiences and emotions are not hard wired.

If a certain feeling – fear – has become connected with heights, you can change that association. You can control your internal world so "calm" equals "heights" or "exciting" equals heights. You have the ability to do that with any event!

Here's another example. If "public speaking" equals "fear," you can change that to "public speaking" equals "excitement," or "fun, "or "confidence," or any other good feeling.

Because your feelings – which make up your internal world – are totally under your control.

Taking Control of Your Internal World

To get yourself moving in a different direction, you're going to have to make changes to your mind and in your body. If you continue to do what you've always done, you're going to get what you have always got. Or to put it another way, here's that well-known definition of "insanity": doing the same thing over and over again and expecting a different result.

To take control of your internal world, all you need to do is change the way you feel in association with any experience.

THREE STEPS TO LEADERSHIP IN YOUR LIFE

There are three things you need to know to take the lead in your life.

1. You need to know where you are.

2. You need to know where you want to go.

3. You need to just do it.

Step 1: You Need to Know Where You Are

If you don't know where you are, it's not possible for you to make any progress.

Here's an example I often give in sessions with clients.

A woman once called me and told me her daughter was getting married in a wedding hall and she wanted to know how to get there. Someone had dropped her off at the wrong wedding hall, and she was frantic.

I asked her, "Where are you? Tell me and I'll tell you how to get to the correct wedding hall."

She answered, "But I can't open my eyes. There's no way I could tolerate the pain of knowing I'm not at my daughter's wedding!"

"But you have to tell me. If you don't tell me, I can't help you."

"But I can't open my eyes. If I open my eyes, there is no way I can tolerate the discomfort."

We were at a stalemate. To get moving again, she needed to tell me where she was at that moment, as painful as that would be for her.

So, it's important to see and know where you are – to see it the way it is, but also not worse than it is.

Step 2: You Need to Know Where You Want to Go

The second step is to see the situation *better* than it is – to see where you want to go. It's important to have a clear image in your mind, because life is controlled by invisible forces, one of which is visualization.

What are some other invisible forces, you may ask? Do I mean gravity? Radio waves? No, what I mean are emotions such as will, rage, optimism, creativity, calmness, and serenity.

You have to take control of these invisible forces in order to shape your life. That's why it's extremely important for you to know where you want to go. Imagery is where you start in accessing the right set of emotions to get into the process of attaining your desired outcome.

Suppose I'm a taxi driver. You get in to my taxi, and I switch on the meter and ask, "Where do you want to go?" If your response is, "Not here – I'm unhappy here," how long is it going to take me to get you to your destination? We could be driving forever because you never gave me an address!

Life is too short to be moving around with no clear direction other than not being where you are now.

Suppose you get in with specific directions of where you *don't* want to go. You say, "Don't take me to New York, don't take me to New Jersey, and don't take me to Pennsylvania." I still have no idea where you want to go, so I still can't effectively take you anywhere.

The quickest and most effective way is for you to get in and say, "I want to go to 25 Park Avenue." Then I can take you there in the quickest possible way.

To get anywhere, you have to know – and be specific and

clear about – where you want to go. There is a specific way to set that up, to be clear about exactly what your destination would look like. It's similar to building a house. You first have to have a picture in your mind of what the end product will look like. From there, you can break it down into the steps that will get you there.

Here's the rule: If you want to get anywhere in your world, you have to know specifically where you want to go so you can clearly map out how to get there.

And to make it the way you see it, to acquire and develop the skills you need, it's a good idea to learn the most effective way to get there from others who have already gotten there. They can direct you and give you the instructions you need to successfully reach your destination. Otherwise, you won't know if you're getting closer or farther away.

Step 3: You Need to Just Do It

The step of just doing it is in your mind.

I would like to share with you a fascinating study pertaining to this idea. The study involves three groups of professional basketball players, and the goal is to see how many baskets each player can make in a row. They're all good players. They all know how to get the ball into the basket. One team practices, one team doesn't practice, and one team practices only in their minds – they imagine shooting the ball into the basket.

Every time this study is done, it turns out the same: The team that wins is the one that practiced in their minds.

Let's analyze how that happens.

- The team that doesn't practice isn't prepared to do well.

- The team that practices on the court gets the ball into the basket a certain number of times – but they also miss a certain number of times, which weakens their confidence and their precision.

- However, the team that practices mentally succeeds with every shot they take. When they get on the floor, they allow their subconscious mind to take control, and they come out ahead.

An enormous part of what professional athletes do is prepare themselves in their minds. This allows their subconscious mind to do what it needs to do. It knows exactly what needs to happen, causing the brain to turn on everything that's needed for a positive outcome.

EXERCISE

Imagining Outcomes Through Your Internal GPS

Here's a simple exercise that you can do in your own home to visualize your desired outcome and its effects.

Your brain has its own internal GPS – when you put a clear address in, it knows how to get you there without your even having to give it directions.

Try this right now.

Stand up with your two feet together, and hold your right hand out, with your pointer finger sticking out straight in front of you.

Now close your eyes.

Turn to your right side without moving your feet out of place, and without moving your right hand away from your body. (If you're left-handed, reverse the instructions. That is, turn to the left, and hold out your left hand and pointer finger.)

With your eyes still closed, turn comfortably to your right. To measure how far you've moved, imagine that you're standing in a clock. In front of you, where you're pointing, is the 12. Behind you is the 6. On the right is the 3, and on the left is the 9. Turn with your eyes closed, then open your eyes and notice where you got to on the clock.

Let's assume you got to 3. Keep that number in mind.

Now, go back to your starting position with your eyes closed and your arm and finger pointing forward. Imagine doing the movements in your mind and going twice as far as you went the first time. But don't actually move yet. Just see yourself doing that. Imagine doing this three times. So if initially you got to 3 o'clock, imagine yourself going to 6 o'clock, twice as far, calmly and easily.

Now attempt to do it again for real. Go as far as you can comfortably go. You will find that you went substantially farther than you did the first time, despite the fact that you didn't do any muscle-relaxing exercises or take any medications to change your physiology.

Now you have experienced the power of learning to control your imagination. It is an amazing power to tap in to, in your body, to be able to control what your body does, just by imagining the desired outcome.

CHANGE THE WAY YOU FEEL

You're working on changing your feelings. The question boils down to this: If you had the exact life you have now but without the feelings that bother you, would you be happy? If you answered yes, then you're in luck, because this is something you can do. You can change the way your feelings are associated with different events in your life, and doing this will prove crucial to your success, even though you're not going to change the specific reality, or the "cold hard facts," of your life.

How you feel is within your control. Through this book you're learning the skills to be able to take back this control. When you take ownership of your emotions, you can make the choice to supercharge yourself and win.

The brain is neutral. You can train it any way you choose. A firewalker trains his brain to be able to walk on hot coals and feel relaxed and confident. A tightrope walker trains his brain to be calm in the face of heights. You can train your brain to be happy or calm, or anything else you choose to experience.

I can prove to you that good feelings do not depend on your circumstances.

As I mentioned before, developmental psychologists say that, by the time we're eight years old, all the emotions we're ever going to experience in life are within us.

If you were told that a parent passed away and then two days later you learned that it was a mistake and your parent was still alive, you would have felt the full experience of losing a parent for those two days just like someone who really had lost a parent. But notice: For you to be sad and to feel those feelings that accompany the death of someone dear, the death doesn't actually have to happen.

And if somebody gave you the positive news that you won the lottery, and two days later it turned out to have been a mistake, for two days you would feel the same feelings as someone who had actually won the lottery.

These feelings are within you now, or, more accurately, you're allowing yourself to experience a feeling that's already in you. What's happening is you are taking a series of different emotions that you already have – sadness, happiness, winning, success, joy, etc. – and putting them together in a certain way to give yourself the emotional experience you have. If someone gets engaged, that person doesn't suddenly develop engagement feelings. They take from within themselves happiness, success, fitness, joy, etc., to conjure up the feeling of being engaged.

So it's clear that any feeling you're going to experience in life already exists within you. You can learn to allow yourself to experience feelings that you already own and have within you that are strong and positive. Why do you need to wait to win the lottery to give yourself permission to be happy? If it's already within you, why don't you instruct yourself today to be just that happy without winning the lottery?

You may ask, rightly, "If it's already in me, why don't I feel it all the time?"

The fact is there are people who do, people who learn how to manage their internal world – the world in which they have total control. You, too, can learn how to access the good feelings that are already in you. You can choose to get up every day with vibrancy, passion, and feelings of success, excitement, and confidence. These feelings are already your gift. You *already* own them. The secret is to learn how to access the emotions and connect them to the events of your day-to-day life.

Some people access the lottery-winning happiness that is pre-wired in them to have that same joy-filled feeling upon waking up in the morning. When they see their family, they attach whatever great feelings they want to experience to that situation. In other words, some people attach amazing feelings to simple events in their lives. In this way, they experience positive emotions most of their lives.

To recap, feelings and situations are not necessarily connected. If I connect the idea that the only way I can feel good is if I'm a millionaire, then I'm cutting myself off from experiencing all the good feelings that I own in my system already. I'm not allowing myself to have these good feelings as a non-millionaire because of a rule that I've imposed on myself.

But I can choose to change that rule so I win the lottery every single morning just by getting out of bed or by doing something else that I do each day. I can have this wonderful experience every single day.

Ultimately, the reason we want to win the lottery is so we can tell our mind that *finally, now*, it has the right to be happy. But we don't need to win the lottery first. Of course, it would be nice for everyone to win the lottery. Financial independence is a beautiful thing. However, we can have the gift of happiness whether we have financial independence or not. (And may we all have financial independence!)

LIMIT YOUR LIMITING FEARS

Emotions have nothing to do with things that go on outside us, or with logic.

The people I meet in my practice clearly understand that their limiting fear doesn't make sense, that it isn't logical. Actually, they feel frustrated and angry when people try to explain to them that their thoughts are irrational. They already know that.

Creativity and Sensitivity in Abundance

People who are limited by their fear aren't weak in the mind. In fact, they possess a recipe made up of two of the most amazing ingredients anyone can own. The same goes for all of us. To have limiting fear we need to be *creative* and we need to be *sensitive*. It takes a lot of creativity to create a fearful image – for example a hungry bear that looks real and scary.

Creativity, the first ingredient, is a wonderful thing. If you're creative, you make the best kind of teacher, friend, employee, or CEO. Anyone who has accomplished anything in the world used their creativity to do it.

Sensitivity, the second ingredient, can make you the best child, the best sibling, the best parent, the best teacher, or the best employee. It's wonderful when you can be sensitive to others. People who are limited by their fear possess an extremely high degree of sensitivity.

And when creativity and sensitivity work together in synergy, great things can evolve.

However, if your creativity is producing a scary bear, and your sensitivity is causing you to run away from the bear you created in your mind, that's a destructive combination. That can blow your life to shambles.

On the other hand, if you can gain control of creativity and sensitivity, then you're in business. You can create positive, beautiful images in your mind. Then, with your sensitivity, you can feel and experience them deeply.

You need to recognize that just as you can be more limited by your fear than most of the world around you, you can also be happier, more excited, more tender, and more loving than most of the world around you.

Just as you can frighten yourself deeply through fearful thoughts, you also can get yourself to feel amazing through imaginative, positive thoughts.

How Do People Develop Limiting Fears?

How do we develop limitations when we have a lot of creativity and sensitivity? The answer is simple. The regular world, including the regular school system, teaches us how to manage a regular degree of creativity and sensitivity.

Let me explain. If you want to learn to drive a car, you can learn from the people around you. But if you want to learn to drive an eighteen-wheel tractor trailer, you've got to get special training and a special license. If your creativity and sensitivity are the size of a car, you can learn how to develop these traits by watching the people around you. But if your creativity and sensitivity are on the order of magnitude of an eighteen-wheeler, you'll need special training to manage it.

And if you're living at the level of a car, accidents will be of the fender-bender variety most of the time. But if you're living at the level of an eighteen-wheeler, accidents will be of the variety in which highways close, everything is in shambles, and people die.

You develop limiting fears when you drive your life with

creativity and sensitivity on the order of magnitude of an eighteen-wheel truck. When you're driving it, it's big and overwhelming, but as long as it's on track, it's fine. As soon as it goes off track, however, that's when your limiting fears make you resistant to the behaviors you need for success.

In my office, I show clients that if they drop a pen, it hardly makes any noise at all, but if they drop a book, it makes a big noise. An average amount of creativity and sensitivity is no big deal when it's out of balance. It is a big deal when you have an abundance of creativity and sensitivity.

Sensitivity is beautiful:

- if you have the knob to turn it up or down,

- if you can turn up the sensitivity when you're around people who make you feel good,

- if you can turn it up when you're receiving a compliment and back down when you're being criticized.

And the same thing is true with creativity. You need – and can develop – the ability to turn up the volume on creativity when you want it and turn it down when you don't.

An abundance of creativity and sensitivity is the biggest blessing of all once you learn how to manage and control it.

KEY 3

MAGNETIZE YOUR THOUGHTS AND ACTIONS

BALANCE PAIN AND GAIN

TWO motivators drive all human behavior and decisions: avoiding pain and seeking pleasure. Therefore, you need to gain control over what you *associate* with pain and what you *associate* with pleasure.

Remember that things, situations, and products don't have any inherent feeling. Everything is neutral. You have a repertoire of feelings you picked up when you were young, and today, as an adult, you can mix and match those feelings to situations. You can decide which feelings go with which situations.

Identifying What to Associate with Pain and Pleasure

Let me show you how this works in your life. Imagine a balance scale that weighs pain and pleasure.

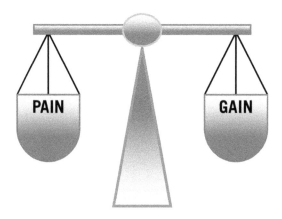

Now imagine that you just woke up, and it's hard for you to get out of bed. It's cold, it's raining, and you're still tired. The balance scale is weighted on the side of "I can't get out of bed."

Then the other side of the balance scale begins to fill up:

- "I don't want to lose a day's pay."

- "My boss is going to be upset."

- "I'm not going to get to school on time."

When this scale ultimately outweighs the other scale, you get out of bed. However if the pain of facing the day remains worse than the pain of staying in bed, you're going to stay in bed.

Here's another scenario. I ask you, "Are you willing to walk ten miles for one dollar?" Your answer is probably no, because the dollar "weighs" less than the ten-mile walk. But what happens if I raise the value of the walk to $100, $250, $500? At some point, that side of the scale is going to weigh more than the pain of walking ten miles and you will do it.

You want to be able to create situations where you clearly associate supercharged actions with pleasure and associate limiting fear and un-resourceful states with pain.

CHANGE YOUR THINKING PATTERNS

Pain is a much stronger motivator than pleasure. You would do a lot more not to lose $10,000 that you already have than to earn $10,000 that you don't have. It's important to recognize the power of avoiding pain.

EXERCISE
"I Want Out of These Situations"

List ten situations you would like to be rid of. Describe the old, painful patterns for each one that you will have to release to succeed. Create enough pain in your descriptions to motivate you to want out, to know you don't want to live in this pattern anymore.

Sometimes this is as simple as creating the opposite of the ten positive images you recorded earlier in this book. Like, "I'll never be able to feel excited and passionate when I get up," or "I'm never going to be able to feel joy, confidence, and drive when I leave the house." Others may be, "I'm never going to have this good relationship," or "I'm never going to be able to attain these good things in my life."

1.

2.

3.

4.

5.

6.

7.

8.

9.

10.

EXERCISE

Imagining a Future with Your Limitations Intact

The previous exercise is not enough to motivate everybody. So here's another one. Visualize what life will look like two years from now if you still have your limitations. How is that going to affect the quality of your schooling, parenting, family life, or work? Use the same ten items as in the exercise above.

1.

2.

3.

4.

5.

6.

7.

8.

9.

10.

Why stop at two years? You can imagine yourself ten or twenty years into the future. The bottom line is, you need to do whatever it takes to create a sense of motivation and urgency to fully appreciate why you must change NOW.

By using the power of imagery to associate fully moving

away from limitations while at the same time moving towards pleasure, you can wire yourself for success and motivation. Why? Because the brain knows how to get you there – it just needs to be motivated and be clearly told where you want to go.

Your brain doesn't know the difference between what's really going on and what's going on in your imagination. If you imagine having many pleasurable emotions, it will interpret that these pleasurable things are actually happening. And after a while, this process will change your thinking patterns.

If you imagine ten positive pictures, twice a day, then after a week, you will have one hundred and forty experiences that are in line with your desired outcome. Before you know it, you have piled enough positive experiences onto the balance scale so that the two sides are equal. It will now become much easier for you to follow through with the choices you want to make in real-world situations.

The Role of Your Choices in Attaining Your Dreams

Associating supercharged actions with pleasure and limiting fear, and un-resourceful states with pain, as you've been doing in this book's exercises, will return your power to choose and to start feeling a sense of control.

The more sense of control that you feel, the less stressed and out of control you feel and the more confident you feel. This will lead you in the direction you want to go.

Cognitive Behavioral Therapy (CBT) has been proven to be the most effective modality for creating lasting, life-enhancing change. CBT helps people break the vicious cycle they're in and overcome problems by identifying and changing unhelpful ways of thinking and behaving.

EXERCISE
How CBT Works

The easiest way to describe how CBT works is through an exercise with a series of diagrams. Here's the first one:

Thoughts	Emotions
Results	Actions

Everything starts with a thought. What you can conceive, you can achieve. When you have a thought, you create an emotion. Draw an arrow from the box labeled thoughts to the box labeled emotions. If your thought was that this is going to work, your emotion may be "hope."

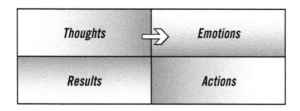

Assuming you have a hopeful emotion, you draw an arrow downward, representing the next step in the cycle. This will drive you to take *action*.

Thoughts	Emotions
Results	Actions

If you do this exercise, chances are you're going to get a result. Draw an arrow from actions to results. If you get a result and you recognize the result, then your belief in that thought is reinforced. You will tell yourself, "This stuff really works. This book is really making a difference in unlocking my potential."

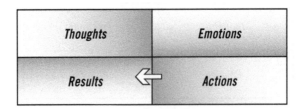

Once you feel that this exercise really works, and you achieve success, your thoughts will be reinforced and your emotion will be even stronger. This will make you take bigger actions and get better results. This is the success cycle. It feeds itself.

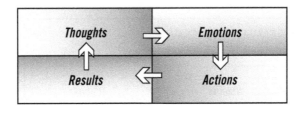

REINFORCE YOUR THOUGHTS

Success Breeds Success

Who is driven to work harder, a poor man or a rich man? The answer is a rich man. Since he has results that reinforce his thoughts, he is much more motivated to get things done.

Who does more research, a professor or a college student? The answer is the professor. Why? Shouldn't the novice student be the one who researches more to learn? No, because the professor already has results. Results reinforce. Results make it easier.

<u>This is why the most important part of the cycle is the arrow that goes from results back to thoughts.</u>

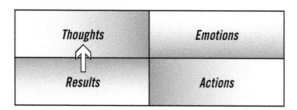

To reinforce your thoughts, you need to acknowledge your results. If you get great results but you discount them, it breaks the cycle.

What to Do About a Broken Cycle

The universe has an invisible negative force that breaks the cycle by discounting a result such that you have to start from scratch and push yourself through the difficulty of making it happen again. All beginnings are difficult, and whoever can beat the system, gets the prize.

CELEBRATE YOUR THOUGHTS

Acknowledging Small Successes

It is important to acknowledge even small successes, because they build into big achievements. If you validate small successes (actions), you get reinforcement (results). If you don't validate the successes, you lack reinforcement, which means it becomes much harder for you to push yourself to go farther.

Why don't people recognize their small successes? Let's use an analogy.

Imagine a teacher who is trying to teach calculus to a three-year-old. The child obviously doesn't have a clue what the teacher is saying. From this you might deduce: the teacher isn't a good teacher, the child isn't smart, or calculus doesn't make any sense. But all of these deductions are wrong. The correct answer is that calculus is not realistically within a child's grasp.

You have to be realistic about your capability.

If you do these exercises and your attitude is, "It's still not better," you ought to check again. If you got 1% better, or even 2% better, that's already an improvement.

Chalk any such improvement up as a success! If you recognize success, you can appreciate it. If you can appreciate it, you can reinforce your thoughts, and success becomes easier. Continue on the success cycle and it will become even easier. You continue the momentum of being able to make progress, and that reinforces the process.

There's a concept in behavioral therapy called *classical*

conditioning, which deals with what we associate with pain and what we associate with pleasure. There's also a concept called *operant conditioning*, which deals with how we will act. That is the behavioral piece, the reinforcement that drives how you feel and affects how you will then act.

Let's take another look at the four boxes. You can directly affect only two sections. Do you know which ones?

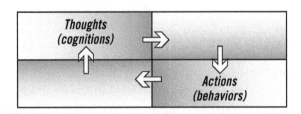

Another word for thought is cognition. Another word for action is behavior. CBT is simply based on the concept of changing your thoughts and actions. It has been proven to be most effective in helping people overcome limitations that rob them of the life they deserve to live. People can learn to apply these skills and supercharge themselves for success. *You* can.

CHANGE YOUR THOUGHTS AND ACTIONS

Let's say someone is afraid he didn't wash his hands properly, and this causes him much distress. He can start by changing his thought and therefore change how he feels so he won't have the need to rewash his hands.

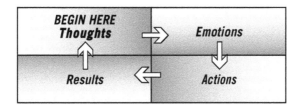

Or he can start by changing his actions. He can purposely not repeat the hand washing, and will discover that nothing happened as a result. That will affect his thoughts, and he won't be as nervous about it next time.

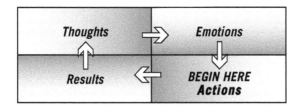

Some limitations are better handled in a behavioral way and others in a cognitive way. The action does not have to be big. What's important is that you set yourself up to make consistent changes. This creates momentum. Change doesn't have to happen in five seconds. You just have to be able to feel and see that you're on the road to progress, that you're consistently getting a sense of control and confidence. This will empower you to continue to do what you need to do to move towards your desired outcome.

Taking action is key. You didn't get where you are today without action, and you're not going to get to a different place without action. And action requires change. Whether you take the cognitive or behavioral approach, it's extremely important for you to make changes. Reinforce the cycle so your thoughts are reinforced and the cycle continues to drive you to your desired outcome.

KEY 4

MANAGE YOUR EMOTIONS

CLAIM YOUR BIRTHRIGHT TO HAPPINESS

I would like to share a cognitive exercise with you that will enable you to change the way you feel and experience the world.

You have to be aware that it's your birthright to be wealthy, happy, fulfilled, and satisfied. Outside factors have no bearing on this – there's abundant proof that wealth, happiness, fulfillment, and satisfaction have nothing to do with circumstances.

Research on lottery winners indicates that a majority of those who win big pretty much destroy their lives. Often those who have fabulous wealth, however they got it, are extremely unhappy. Moreover, there are people who have very little but are extremely satisfied and happy.

In 2009, an iconic pop singer died. His album sales had broken records, with one of them still the best-selling album of all time. In his own way, he made a substantial difference in the world. But he died at age fifty because he was taking so many drugs to raise his mood, wake him up, put him to sleep – and all this finally caused a cardiac arrest.

He was not happy. He was miserable. How could this be? He had everything going for him. Or did he?

The Saga of W. Mitchell

In contrast, there is the amazing W. Mitchell.

One day, he was flying a plane, solo, which is a freeing and exhilarating experience. Right after he was done, he got on his motorcycle, in somewhat of a trance.

Mitchell suddenly realized that he was about to crash into a box truck. Instinctively, he slid his motorcycle under the truck. Unfortunately, his bike's gas cap came off, and friction caused the gas to ignite. Mitchell was caught in a ball of fire until somebody coming out of a local car dealership saved him by extinguishing the flames. Sixty-five percent of his body was severely burned. He lost his fingers. He woke up two to three weeks later in the burn unit in extreme pain. It even hurt to breathe.

He describes what he thought to himself as he was lying there. "Look. I can choose to think about what's bothering me and be miserable, or I can make the decision to focus on what's good about life." He said he didn't see it as a choice. He went on to learn how to use his skin-grafted hands and live his life fully.

In fact, he went on to become the number-one employer in the state of Vermont and reach multimillionaire status. Within eight years he was married and had retired to a small town in Colorado. He was really enjoying his life.

Mitchell owned his own airplane and loved the adventure of flying. One day he invited some friends to go out with him. As the plane took off, he realized that things were not looking good, so he crash-landed. His friends jumped out of the airplane, but he wasn't able to. Now he was paralyzed from the waist down.

When he was in the hospital, people said, "Remember you used to say it's not what happens to you, it's what you do about it? Focus on the good."

"That's not for me!" he replied. "That's for people with one problem. I have multiple problems, and now I'm paralyzed from the waist down! There is no way I can think positive in this situation."

But he realized that he had to. So he found a new way of looking at the world. He used to be able to do ten thousand things but realized that now he could do only nine thousand things. The choice that faced him was to focus on the one thousand things he *couldn't* do or on the nine thousand things he *could* do. He knew that out of these, if he could do a couple of hundred things well, he would have a great life.

W. Mitchell went on to become the mayor of his city; he ran for Lieutenant Governor of Colorado and today is an extremely wealthy, successful motivational speaker. By focusing on what is working in his life, he's one of the happiest people on the face of the earth.

CREATE POSITIVE THOUGHTS AND FEELINGS

If you experience limiting negative emotions, that means you have creativity and sensitivity in abundance. You have the equivalent of a top-of-the-line IMAX-grade HD screen with surround sound in your brain. How you feel at any given moment depends on what movie you put into the play deck of your brain.

If you play happy thoughts, you're going to have extremely happy feelings. If you play excited thoughts, you're going to have amazing feelings of excitement. If you play sad thoughts, you're going to have very sad thoughts.

Think about it. If you're at a funeral, wearing headphones and watching a video of something funny, you're going to feel like laughing – despite the fact that a funeral is going on around you. If you're sitting at a wedding and watching a sad experience, you're going to feel sad.

W. Mitchell plays happy thoughts in his mind, and the pop singer played miserable thoughts in his. You need to get control of your mind. You need to play thoughts that make you feel wealthy, happy, fulfilled, and satisfied. The way you do this is by creating positive thoughts and feelings in your mind – in both a qualitative and quantitative way.

Let's first talk about a qualitative way. Come up with something in your life that you could be grateful for but currently are not. For example, you have no trouble with your vision, but probably don't have any appreciation for it. What if you lost your vision, but luckily, two years later, surgery restored it for you? You would almost certainly be very grateful to have your sight back, and little things wouldn't bother you. The whole world would look beautiful to you, so who cares about the idiot who cut you off in traffic? What's important is that you can see again.

Did you wake up feeling excited this morning about being able to see? Why not? If someone who lost his vision for two years is excited and feels blessed that he can see, you're even more blessed than he is. Not only can you see today, but you were spared from two years of vision loss. Shouldn't you be even more joyful about being blessed with sight?

The reason you're not is that you have become habituated to sight. You need to learn how to continually "supercharge your emotions" to facilitate positive feelings.

Specifically, you have to learn how to add positive emotions to good thoughts and take negative emotions away from bad thoughts. Emotions are like magnets. They get stuck. You can learn how to magnetize good thoughts so they stick in your mind, and how to demagnetize bad thoughts. Imagine your brain as a metal basket that thoughts go in and out of all day. The thoughts that are going to stick are the magnetic thoughts, that is, the thoughts that have emotions attached to them.

EXERCISE
Strengthening Your Gratitude Attitude

Try this. Pick something in your life that is going well but that you don't pay much attention to. Now deeply feel the emotion of appreciation within yourself. Continue to access that feeling of gratitude and focus on intensifying the emotion that you're feeling. You're now experiencing the process of magnetizing a thought. Continue this exercise for a week, concentrating on the items that you are grateful for. Make a list of ten items. Write them down and fully associate with them daily.

1.

2.

3.

4.

5.

6.

7.

8.

9.

10.

Use more than one sense as you associate with each. How does it feel?

Next, go back to the ten items you just wrote and fully associate positive emotions for all ten of them every day for the next week. The more you associate the good feelings, the stronger the magnetized thought will become. These areas of your life will now evoke a magnetized supercharged emotion.

Raising your level of happiness in life will begin when you begin to generate more good feelings with your thoughts.

Happiness comes from the success of overcoming your limitations. Happiness is not "pleasure." Happiness is progress and victory.

Happiness does not come from what you own. Your true assets are actually your problems, because they're what will be giving you good feelings. They're going to make you feel that you're making progress; they're going to give you a sense of victory.

Issues and problems are your keys to happiness, joy, and satisfaction. G-d in His infinite wisdom knows exactly what problem to give you to help empower you so you can enjoy life so much more.

Success Against All Odds

The following story is about a couple by the name of Smith.

The Smiths had a child who was born with cerebral palsy. After his birth, the doctors told them not to bother taking the child home, that he wouldn't be able to develop properly. There seemed to be little hope for this child.

The Smiths decided that they would reject the doctor's recommendations. They wanted to take the child home.

Later they were told of a Dr. Goldstein in Chicago who might be able to help them, and they set up an appointment to meet with him.

Dr. Goldstein administered a battery of tests on the child. He then met with the parents to debrief them on the results. His assessment was that the child would never walk again, but that, with intense therapy, over time he might have the ability to sit and develop some of his motor skills.

The parents felt a sense of hope and were prepared to do whatever was necessary to help their child.

Two years later, the mother called the father at work and excitedly told him to come home. When he got there, he found the child lying on a mat in a puddle of sweat. With an overwhelming feeling of joy he witnessed his child move.

The couple's dedication to their son and the therapy had finally paid off.

Years later, at his bar mitzvah, the boy gave an outstanding speech. What's even more incredible is that he is on a hockey team, totally functional – and living as a healthy, normal child.

Was the father happier because his child conquered cerebral

palsy than he would have been if he had had a child without a serious health issue?

The enormous emotional sense of progress and of victory is what made the father happier. His true happiness was intrinsically linked to the success of overcoming a problem.

You will become a stronger and happier person when you meet your challenges and fears head-on. When you conquer them, you will feel a great sense of victory and happiness that will naturally dominate your emotions.

The entire journey you must travel will be worth it at the end because of the person you will become.

MAKE HAPPINESS A HABIT

You have the ability to magnetize dormant things in your life, making them stronger so you experience good feelings.

The reason we don't appreciate our eyes, our family, our health, our clothing is that we're used to them. We take them for granted. This is explained by the concept of *habituation*, our tendency to get used to things that are good. This is how we get past feeling uncomfortable in new surroundings or wearing new clothes: we get used to it.

Basically, we can habituate to almost anything, whether positive or negative. If we get a new car, we get used to it within a few weeks. The challenge, as set out in this book, is to take control of that process, by:

- habituating to the bad things, the things we don't want to experience, that make us stressed and anxious, and

- "un-habituating" to the things we like, things that feel good, things that will empower us.

By habituating to the bad things, we can magnetize positive emotions to ourselves, which will overcome our stress. By un-habituating to good things, we can avoid taking for granted the positives of our life, and feel great all the time.

Let's talk about a common challenge that many of us face, the challenge of getting to the place where we feel good about ourselves, our situations, and our surroundings. This leads us to the category of positive thinking, or positive psychology.

You need to evaluate the following: How do you treat yourself? How do you talk to yourself? How do you think to yourself?

The Bible says, "Love your friend like yourself." Inherent in the verse is the message that you have to treat yourself *like* your friend. If your friend was down or stressed, you wouldn't say, "You're a loser; you're never going to get better," would you? That means you can't say it to *yourself* if you're down or stressed.

You need to talk to yourself the way you would talk to a friend you care about and want to help. If you accept yourself the way G-d accepts you, then you will realize that you really have a good essence, because there's not one person in the world who doesn't have many positive qualities.

Much research has been done to prove the power of intention and our ability to affect our world and what will manifest in it. Namely, experts like Dr. Wayne Dyer and documentaries like *The Secret* have utilized science to prove the inner power we have through our thoughts to change, create, and manifest reality in our lives.

To begin, you need to develop a belief that negative emotions and negative thoughts offer no benefit, that they're never worth engaging in. Every emotion is preceded by a thought. The quality of your thoughts, which are driven by the questions you ask yourself, will therefore shape the emotion you experience.

To sum up, you're a living magnet. You attract into your life what's in harmony with your dominant thoughts.

Since, as mentioned in the chapter on Key 1, there is no erasing of any memories from your brain, you can add only positive thoughts. And the more positive thoughts you have, the better and the stronger emotionally you'll be. You'll also learn how to handle thoughts so one bad thought doesn't knock you down and spark a pattern of negativity.

I learned this concept from a phlebotomist at a time when I was fearful of having my blood drawn. I actually avoided buying life insurance because I could not handle the thought of giving blood. Finally, one insurance agent told me, "I'm going to send a phlebotomist to you and the experience will be easy so you won't have an issue."

The phlebotomist arrived and took my blood, and I had absolutely no problem with it. I was curious about what she had done to get me to feel okay about something I had feared so much. "It's simple," she said. "I talked to you to keep your mind occupied."

The mind can move fast, but it can think only one thought at a time. Therefore, <u>if you learn how to manage your thoughts, you can feel differently. If your current thoughts create stress and limitation, you can replace them with empowering thoughts.</u>

The Power of Your Mind

Dr. Deepak Chopra conducted a study in 2009 and 2010 in New York City in which he interviewed doctors with terminally ill patients. These were doctors who had to tell their patients how long they were going to live.

Dr. Chopra wanted to measure the percentage of people who died exactly on the day on which they had been told they were going to die, whether it was sixty days or ninety days or some other period. His findings revealed the percentage to be 85%. When people believe and trust that they're going to die by a certain day, a significant number of them die on that day.

And the opposite is often the case, too, because the power of positivity works in a similar way. Many studies show how a positive attitude can defy medical odds. Our thoughts hold a tremendous, life-altering power that can also play an important role in our well-being.

<u>Our thoughts are basically dictated by questions.</u>

You always ask yourself questions, such as, "What does this mean?" "How's it going to go?" "Am I fine?" "Am I not fine?" "Is it going to be okay?"

<u>Learn how to ask yourself good questions to get better answers.</u>

Ask your brain a question, and you will get an answer. If your brain doesn't have the answer, it will make one up.

Ask yourself, "What's good about my life?" and you'll get an answer. If you ask, "What's bad about my life?" you'll also get an answer.

If you ask, "What's good about my family?" you'll get an answer. Ask, "What's bad about my family?" and you'll get an answer to that question, too.

Every question also makes an assumption. In other words, if you ask, "Will my anxiety ever go away?" your assumption is that it might not. Because the assumption is in your subconscious, it doesn't get questioned.

Notice the difference when the question is asked this way: "When will my anxiety go away?" What's the assumption here? That the anxiety is going to go away.

Which of the two questions do you think is going to have a better result?

EXERCISE

Focusing on What Works

Two times a day for a week, perhaps in the morning and the evening, write down ten things that you're thankful for. How about that cup of coffee you had this morning or that person who was kind to you at the grocery store? Perhaps something tangible such as a shirt that makes you feel good when you wear it. Try not to repeat the same item because you want to come up with as many items as you can to be thankful for. So one cup of coffee can make it on your list only once.

This challenge becomes even more powerful after the first few days, because all the things you can think of will quickly get used up and now you really have to think. This is the breakthrough point, the point at which you start to really activate your brainpower.

Remember, every single time you ask yourself that question, two things happen:

1. you're going to get an answer, and

2. you're making an assumption that there is something else that's good about your life, your family, your neighborhood, as well as many other things.

You're essentially forcing your brain into a pattern of asking what else is good about your life.

You're forcing your brain to focus on the part of your life that works.

DAY 1
Morning

1.

2.

3.

4.

5.

6.

7.

8.

9.

10.

11.

12.

13.

14.

15.

16.

17.

18.

19.

20.

DAY 2
Morning

21.

22.

23.

24.

25.

26.

27.

28.

29.

30.

Evening

31.

32.

33.

34.

35.

36.

37.

38.

39.

40.

DAY 3
Morning

41.

42.

43.

44.

45.

46.

47.

48.

49.

50.

Evening

51.

52.

53.

54.

55.

56.

57.

58.

59.

60.

DAY 4
Morning

61.

62.

63.

64.

65.

66.

67.

68.

69.

70.

Evening

71.

72.

73.

74.

75.

76.

77.

78.

79.

80.

DAY 5
Morning

81.

82.

83.

84.

85.

86.

87.

88.

89.

90.

Evening

91.

92.

93.

94.

95.

96.

97.

98.

99.

100.

DAY 6

Morning

101.

102.

103.

104.

105.

106.

107.

108.

109.

110.

Evening

111.

112.

113.

114.

115.

116.

117.

118.

119.

120.

DAY 7
Morning

121.

122.

123.

124.

125.

126.

127.

128.

129.

130.

Evening

131.

132.

133.

134.

135.

136.

137.

138.

139.

140.

BREAK YOUR NEGATIVE THOUGHT PATTERNS

Negativity fuels more negativity in your thought patterns. Feelings of frustration, anger, hostility, irritability, and so on do not evoke a positive response.

You can cause a feel-good attitude just by accessing what you're grateful for in your life. Try it next time you're feeling negative emotions.

Seeing the World Through Rose-Colored Glasses (or Not!)

Distortions are what drive your negative views of the world and set up your limitations. Your view of the world is different compared with another person's view.

When people come to my office I use a metaphor to get this point across. I ask them, "What color is the light in the ceiling?" They answer "yellow" or "white."

Then I take out eight different pairs of sunglasses. I put a blue pair of sunglasses on them and I ask again, "What color is the light?" Of course, they say "blue."

And so on with red, yellow, and green.

The response is always based on the color they see. Then I ask, "Why are you telling me blue, red, yellow. and green? Do you think that because I put a piece of plastic in front of your eyes the color of the light actually changes?"

Logically, they know that the light didn't change. What's happening is that their brain is seeing it in a distorted way.

If you see your life through black glasses, you will believe everything is black, even though in your mind you know that some things are perhaps white. Emotions are driven by the way you see them; they're driven by the glasses you look through to see the world.

The goal is to take off your colored glasses so you can see the world the way it really is.

Most people, if they see the world through clear glasses, find the world is tolerable. G-d gave us the ability to accept and appreciate our actual world. And it turns out that the world's a beautiful place when we see the big picture.

How do you recognize your distortions so you can begin to see the world in a clear way? By learning how to capture your automatic thoughts.

EXERCISE

Capturing Your Automatic Thoughts

On each day of the next week record three automatic thoughts that you've had that day. Your challenge is simply to catch the thoughts and record them.

You have learned that every emotion is preceded by a thought. For example, if you're feeling down, you need to ask yourself, "What thought have I been thinking?"

What did you think?

- "I'm no good."

- "It's never going to work."

- "I'm a loser."

- "This is never going to go away."

- "Someone is going to be angry at me."

Whatever it is, recognize the automatic thought and write it down. Challenge yourself to have twenty-one thoughts written down by the end of the week.

Day 1

    1.

    2.

    3.

Day 2

    1.

    2.

    3.

Day 3

    1.

    2.

    3.

Day 4

    1.

    2.

    3.

Day 5

    1.

    2.

3.

Day 6

   1.

   2.

   3.

Day 7

   1.

   2.

   3.

Go back through your list and ask yourself if the thoughts are accurate. For example, are the thoughts "I'm not good" or "I'm never going to make it" the truth?

Most of the time you'll find that the thought is inaccurate, that it's just an exaggerated and distorted way of seeing something.

Distorted Thoughts

As you complete the chart above, it will help you to consider the ten most common negative distortions experienced by people with limitations, as follows.

Distortion 1: All-or-Nothing Thinking

If you're a perfectionist, there's no 99% in your vocabulary. If something isn't 100%, it's a zero. For you, if a performance isn't perfect, it's a total failure. When things are good, they're good. The moment they're not, then everything is wrong.

Perfectionists are saddled with many limitations. They may have a friend, but the second the person does something a little unfriendly, their response is, "That person hates me." Their attitude is that if you like me, you'll always do what I want. If you don't, it means you don't like me. And if you don't like me, it means you hate me.

There's no middle ground. There's no gray area. This kind of thinking can't tolerate ambivalence.

Distortion 2: Overgeneralizing

A single negative event is viewed as a perpetual pattern: "You always do this to me." Even though many times they don't, it still gets generalized. So instead of just saying, "You did this," or "I did this," or "I failed," the negative events become perpetual patterns.

Distortion 3: Filtering Out Positives

You focus on a single negative detail until your vision of reality is blurred, like a drop of ink that discolors an entire beaker of water. You focus so hard on the negative things that everything else falls away.

I work with an extremely successful educator who has been at the helm of a large, successful school for years and years. He made one mistake, and now he focuses on that mistake. He no longer can see himself as qualified to do that job.

That's how the mental filter distortion works. You filter out everything else that happened before. This negative event distorts your reality, and that is how you see yourself.

Distortion 4: Disqualifying the Positive

You reject positive experiences by insisting that they don't count, even though this is contradicted by actual experiences. You do this in order to maintain a negative belief.

You might say, "I'm such a bad husband." To which someone

points out some of the good things you have done. "Nah, that doesn't mean anything," you say.

You disqualify all the positive things that contradict your negative feeling in order to stay with your negative feeling.

People with limitations and fears very often disqualify the positive.

Distortion 5: Jumping to Conclusions, or Fortune Telling

You offer negative interpretations of events, even though there are no definite facts that convincingly support that conclusion. I sometimes refer to this as the little man in your head who predicts negative things about to happen.

If people looked at how many times their negative conclusions came true, they'd realize that they wouldn't invest a penny with someone on Wall Street with a track record like theirs! We tend to have this automatic negative interpretation of events, even though there's no fact that convincingly supports that conclusion.

You know, an optimist and a pessimist are both liars, because neither of them has any idea of what's going to happen. The only difference is, the pessimist is a liar who has a miserable life and the optimist is a liar who has a good life.

Someone who jumps to conclusions has no idea what the future's going to bring but thinks like this:

- "I'm going to go on an airplane, and the plane's going to crash."

- "Things aren't going to pan out."

- "I'm going to mess up."

This person really has no reason to believe that it's going to happen that way. There's no past performance that dictates it.

Distortion 6: Mindreading

You think that people are seeing you negatively. You misread messages and take them personally. Someone coughs when you say something, and you interpret it as a hidden message. You believe you have the power to read other people's minds, but all this does is cause you a lot of social distress.

It's important for people to understand this distortion, especially those who have social limitations. You really have no idea what other people are thinking. You really have no idea if their thoughts are positive or negative.

Dr. David Burns conducted a study (one that I have replicated in my own office) in which he had some of the best clinicians in the world fill out how depressed a client was after a therapy session and how much they felt they understood their client. And he had the clients fill out the questionnaire, too, assessing themselves emotionally before and after the session.

Believe it or not, Dr. Burns found that the therapist and the client were on the same page only 10% of the time. That means, for example, a client could leave a session and achieve results towards their goal even though their therapist felt the session was a failure! Or it could be the other way around.

If the best clinicians in the world are right only 10% of the time, you can be assured that the accuracy of your mindreading isn't any better. You have no sure idea what other people are thinking.

Distortion 7 Magnifying and Minimizing

You exaggerate your errors and downplay your achievements. You emphasize imperfections and underestimate talent.

It's as if you take a pair of binoculars and, looking through one side, you see a beauty mark or birthmark or some imperfection as so big and obvious it makes you feel you are ugly. You look at one of your attributes – for example, your negativity – and that's all you see about yourself.

Then you look through the other side of the binoculars at all the good things about yourself, your beautiful attributes, all your beautiful features, and you can barely see them.

Another word for this is catastrophizing. Someone who is nervous about flying in an airplane views the risk of crashing and maximizes it. The same person may feel safe driving a car, yet four hundred thousand people die in car accidents in a year while very few die on commercial airplanes.

This distortion boils down to the fact that when you minimize and magnify, you don't experience things as they really are.

Distortion 8: Reasoning Emotionally

You assume that your negative emotions represent reality. "This is how I feel, so it must be true." If you think someone hates you, if you think something's dangerous, if you think you're not well, you believe that what you think represents reality.

<u>Anyone with limitations gives their emotions way too much credibility.</u>

The truth is, emotions can come up for what seems like no reason whatsoever. They can come from something called an anchor. For example, if you were somewhere and felt bad every time you happened to be there and found yourself in that situation again, you would probably feel bad – even though there is nothing in the *present* situation to make you feel this way.

Just because you may feel something doesn't necessarily mean it's true. A person can feel chest pains and think they're having a heart attack, but this does not automatically mean they're having a heart attack. The number-one diagnosed disorder in emergency rooms in the United States is panic disorder.

The following is what this distortion leads to.

- If you think you're not good, it must be you're not good.

- If you think you're not worthy, you're not worthy.

- If you think you're not worthy of love, you're not worthy of love.

Distortion 9: Bowing to the "Should" Statement

"I should do this," "I ought to do this." Who said so? You may carry this sense of obligation due to the programming you received from parents, teachers, or "society." "Should" makes you feel angry, frustrated, and resentful. An emotional consequence of "should" and "ought" is guilt.

If you say to yourself that you should do something, ask yourself, "Who says I should?"

If you make yourself do something that you want to do, that will move you towards your goals in life and obviously that's good. But if you recognize that it's just a "should" that moves you away from where you want to go, you need to recognize it as a distortion. And if it's a distortion, you can:

- take off that pair of glasses,

- feel how the "should" or the "must" or the "ought to" does something to you that's dysfunctional, and

- get on towards your goals in life.

Distortion 10: Labeling and Mislabeling

This is an extreme form of overgeneralization, which I spoke of earlier, under Distortion 2. Instead of focusing on the fact that you made an error, you transfer the negativity to yourself. In other words, it's not that I made a mistake or I messed up. It's that I'm a loser.

Mislabeling involves describing an event with highly colored and emotionally loaded language.

- "He's a liar."

- "She's such a loser."
  Very loaded statements.

Obviously when you label or mislabel someone – including yourself – it's inaccurate. Parenting workshops emphasize the importance of not mislabeling kids. There's a big difference between saying, "You did something bad" and saying, "You're a bad kid." When kids hear the latter from their parents, they adopt that label, which can affect them negatively, sometimes for the rest of their life.

You may have grown up being labeled. You have to be able to see yourself and recognize that it's just a distortion.

Distortion 11: Personalizing

You see yourself as the cause of some negative external event for which, in fact, you're not primarily responsible. You personalize, and it's a distortion. You don't really affect *anything* directly. You have no idea what actually causes what. If you think you're affecting an outside, external event, it will have an impact on the quality of your life, because you will base your actions on that perception.

EXERCISE

Detecting the Distortions in Your Automatic Thoughts

Now go back through your list of automatic thoughts earlier in this chapter and take each one of them through the following three-column grid, figuring out which distortion of the eleven just discussed is involved in the thought and what the true thought is.

1	2	3
The Automatic Thought	The Distortion Behind the Thought	The True Thought

In column number 1, write down your automatic thought. Example: "I always mess up," or "I'm such a bad person."

Now go through possible distortions: Am I being all or nothing? Am I a perfectionist? Am I always a bad person?

Now recognize that you're not. It's not all or nothing. Sometimes you're a good person.

Ask yourself if you're:

- overgeneralizing, or

- filtering, or

- disqualifying the positive that you do, or

- jumping to conclusions, or

- magnifying or minimizing, or

- using emotional reasoning – believing that because you feel that way, that's the way it is, or

- mindreading – thinking that people don't like you, or

- saying to yourself that you should do something, even though that's really not the case, or

- labeling yourself.

One or more of these can apply to your automatic thought. For example, at one time you may be using emotional reasoning and at another time you may be an all-or-nothing thinker.

Now write the distortion in the middle column. For example, "I'm doing all-or-nothing thinking," or "I'm using emotional reasoning," or "I'm mindreading."

The third column is for your new thought – the one that will bring about an important change for you.

You may find this a bit more challenging because you're wearing those distorting glasses. The best way to come up with a new thought would be to see yourself as if you were an outsider. If a friend of yours did what you did and asked you, "Am I really such a loser?" what would you tell him? You'd say, "Nah, you just feel like a loser because..." Then you would record the distortion: "...because you're being all or nothing" or "...because you're mindreading other people."

When you do this as if you're a third party, it's easier for you to see things more rationally. So the new thought might be, "Sometimes I make a mistake, but so many times I do such great things."

The automatic thought that you put in the first column, "I always mess up," is how you actually feel it and experience it. But the truth is in the third column: "Sometimes I make mistakes."

Bringing a distortion to your awareness is what releases it.

Once you recognize your automatic thought, you work through and recognize the distortions that are making you view the situation like that, causing you to feel and experience your world in a particular way.

Recognizing the truth and putting it in the third column – "I make mistakes, sometimes, but 95% of the time, I get it right, and I'm actually very successful" – makes your life much more tolerable. Actually, much better than tolerable, because now you can live, really live, by the truth.

The Effect of Distortions on Automatic Thoughts

You need to be able to recognize when you're seeing the world in a distorted way. If you're like most people, you'll discover that the same three or four distortions are involved in most of your negative thoughts. These distortions are the glasses that you wear. You see everything this way.

I talked about grabbing and looking at three automatic negative thoughts a day. The reason they're so powerful is that they're automatic. We don't question automatic thoughts.

However, an automatic thought can be a beautiful thing. Because when your positive thought exercises kick in, your automatic thoughts and feelings will be good ones without you having to sit down and think about it.

You want to set yourself up to have automatic positive thoughts, short-circuiting the pattern of automatic negative thoughts.

Recognizing Distortions Unlocks Your Inaccurate View

Once you recognize and create a statement in the third column, your brain will be able to unlock your true potential. It will realize that what you experience is not necessarily what your reality is. This awareness unlocks your belief, your understanding, and your view of the world.

From what we have discussed in this book so far, and the exercises you have filled out, the door is now opening, allowing you to access a refreshing perspective of the world – a world that seems like a much happier place. You now can begin to identify your positive attributes and recognize how to ask good questions of yourself and how to get better outcomes. Your smokescreen of distortions is beginning to dissipate.

MAKE CORRECT CHOICES

As you continue your journey towards the life you desire and deserve, begin to recognize the power G-d gives you to choose and make decisions. It is possibly your most precious asset. Your destiny takes form as you make decisions.

The knowledge that you have the power to make decisions is the foundation of manifesting your personal power. Self-esteem is built on the fact that you have the power to control your destiny, and that the more you exercise this power, the more it is reinforced in your understanding and emotional experience. Self-esteem is what makes you feel empowered and gives you the strength to follow through on the choices and decisions you make.

True self-esteem comes from reinforcing the belief that your decisions and actions do make a difference, from affirming that you are in control by making choices and following through.

You will make mistakes and wrong choices occasionally. That's part of the process.

In order to develop your decision-making muscles, you need to make choices and act on them. The more you use these muscles, the bigger they grow and the more confident you will be using them. The more good choices you make, the higher your self-esteem will grow. The more you believe in your personal power, the more you accomplish and the more you will love yourself.

Anxiety and stress are generated from just the opposite. They spring from the feeling of being out of control. When people feel out of control, they cannot tolerate the pain. And unless they hold the right skill set to deal with these feelings, they will take the easiest and most widely used way out, running away from the pain.

And because what they desire in life is usually attached to some level of pain, running away from pain in essence is running away from life.

Let me explain. Is it easier to be in a relationship with another person who has needs, wants, desires, feelings, and opinions, or to just live by yourself? Is it easier to have the responsibility of a job or a department or even owning your own business or be homeless and live off handouts? Is it easier to have children who come with emotional, financial, and physical needs, or just live and take care of yourself?

The answer is that you don't want what is easier, at least when you're thinking with reason and logic. However, unfortunately, if you don't manage your emotions, they will control you and cause you to begin making bad choices. Basically, it's like forgoing what you desire in the long haul and what will bring you deep joy and satisfaction just to get relief from your pain in the short term.

So if everything you desire and hold valuable in life is glued to pain, you need to learn how to effectively manage your emotions so you can move in the direction you have decided to follow. This is how you will achieve your dreams.

The world offers many effective negative strategies to help you avoid pain and run away from life. Some of them seem good, given the effect they can have, but then there is the possibility that you will become addicted to them. Addiction is a pleasure that numbs pain. One of the biggest pains our society runs away from is the pain of low self-esteem, which stems from not feeling in control of one's life.

One horrific example is suicide. This is the ultimate way to run away from life and pain. In a survey, twenty-six thousand college students were asked if they ever contemplated suicide to relieve them of their troubles. Incredibly, more than half said yes.

Addictions come in many forms. They usually involve substances such as drugs, alcohol, inappropriate materials, relationships, movies, and the Internet.

If your self-esteem is low and you don't feel happy with yourself, you may begin to distract yourself by becoming lazy, too busy, or by turning to pleasures such as drugs or food. These things give you a feeling of control because they begin to make you feel better.

Another short-term negative coping strategy for surviving the internal torture of low self-esteem is to try to please others and seek their approval faking an ego. This generates a feeling of self-worth as you begin to like yourself better because other people like you. Over time, however, you begin to feel out of control because you have no control over whether people like you or not.

One big pain that holds people back from making good choices and following through is the possibility of making mistakes and experiencing an even bigger pain. However, making mistakes is the only way to go. Why? Because success is the product of good judgments, good judgments are the product of experience, and experience is the product of bad judgment.

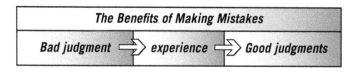

Albert Einstein said it very clearly: "Anyone who has never made a mistake has never tried anything new." Emotional mastery skills are required to deal with unavoidable challenge in the process of moving towards goals and aspirations.

You need to take full responsibility for your life so you

can develop your self-esteem and take the actions needed to succeed. When you're happy, calm, and confident and love yourself, you can accomplish your goals and aspirations much more easily. The process of making good choices requires that you choose to break habits that do not serve you and the life that you want to live. To accomplish this, you need to create momentum to break the force or else rationalizations will kick in.

All your faculties and abilities come into play when you have something you *must* do. Think about it. Have you ever gone out without your clothing, even when you're in an extreme rush? Have you ever relieved yourself in your clothes in the middle of the street, even when you were really desperate? Of course not. Meeting the musts that go with self-respect and social acceptability is ingrained in you.

Turn your SHOULDS into MUSTS and raise your standards. Don't be willing to settle for anything less.

A big obstacle to making choices and not taking responsibility is procrastination, which is basically the fear of success. People procrastinate because they're afraid of the success that they know will result if they move ahead now. Success is heavy and carries responsibility. It is much easier to live in a "someday" mindset. It's just another tactic for avoiding the pain of life, which is glued to any worthwhile desire or goal.

To heal your emotional issues and develop emotional muscles, you need to work on them daily.

Action is what got you here in the first place. Here are some fascinating stats: Research shows that:

- 100% of people will experience anxiety in their lifetime, but only 18% will develop anxiety disorder.

- 100% of people will experience despair, sadness, loss, and depression, but only 9.5% will suffer clinical depression.

- 60-80% will experience a significant trauma, but only 6-8% will develop PTSD.

- 2-35% of people will have panic attacks, yet only 2.7% will have panic disorder.

- Most people experience fear, but only 6-8% will develop phobias.

These experiences evolve and progress into a disorder when you change a behavior to accommodate the fear. Don't make the wrong choice of letting a negative emotion spiral into a disorder.

It's a good idea, when you start taking responsibility for your choices, to start with the easy and then move on to the difficult. One example would be to work on your physical body and then on your emotions. Your mind and body are intertwined, and changes in one realm will directly affect the other realm.

Managing Thoughts and Actions

Now let's put it all together and develop the skills for emotional mastery.

To this point we have focused on understanding *why* we need to have mastery in order to supercharge our emotions to win. This is 80% of the equation. Trying to succeed without knowing the why is the equivalent of setting out for a road trip with no destination in mind. Most people live without any idea of where they're headed. The famous quote from John Beckley holds true as ever…"Most people don't plan to fail: they fail to plan."

Many simply live life with no plan; they just keep on moving ahead with no goals. That explains why most people don't live the life they dream of living.

As Vince Lombardi put it, "The difference between a successful person and others is not a lack of strength, not a lack of knowledge, but rather a lack of will."

So it is vitally important that you understand the why. But it is time now for you to advance to the 20% of the equation, which is the *how*.

You have an inner power, a part of you that is G-dly and unlimited. It is perfect and it has the power to cure you from illness. It has the ability to bring anything you want into your life. Bob Proctor says, "Thoughts become things. If you see it in your mind, you will hold it in your hand."

Your external body is the most amazing creation on earth and it has amazing capabilities. Famous people such as Albert Einstein and Margaret Mead have been quoted as stating a variation of the idea that we use only about 10% of our brains. Regardless of the body's purely scientific value, people have tapped in to its unlimited potential to achieve goals beyond their colleagues' expectations. It is possible.

Your task is to facilitate the creation of a bridge between the limitless super power that is within you and the most amazing and powerful creation, your body. If you can bridge the gap, all limitations melt away and you can realize your dreams, goals, and aspirations.

The bridge you need to create is composed of two components: your thoughts and your actions. Through your thoughts and actions, you bridge the gap and allow your unlimited potential to cross over into your physical experience and manifest itself in your life.

Earlier I discussed how your thoughts affect your emotions. Based on your emotions, you can take or not take any action, thereby affecting your result or manifestation.

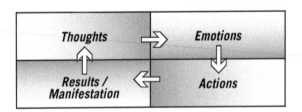

The management of your thoughts has been a significant part of this discussion and the exercises up to this point. The benefit of the exercises has been two-fold: to help you create new neurological pathways in your brain towards pleasure and desired outcomes and to help you to stop using current limiting and stress-provoking pathways and instead reinforce new and desired patterns.

Both abundance and lack exist simultaneously in your life as parallel realities. Which secret garden you will tend is always a conscious choice. When you choose not to focus on what's missing from your life and instead to be grateful for the abundance that's present in life – love, health, family, friends, work, the joys of nature, and personal pursuits that bring you pleasure – the wasteland of illusion falls away and we experience heaven on earth.

If you own a television, you can choose the channel you want to watch. You have the free will to decide whether to expose yourself to something funny, sad, or even frightening. You recognize your control to tune in to the station that serves you and makes you feel better. So, too, in your life there are many channels: trauma, sadness, depression, and frustration, but also, confidence, empowerment, love, passion, happiness, success, wealth, and many more.

Too many people have a list of things that they need to do or have before they can be happy. How many times have you said or thought, "I'll be happy when…?" as if, in time, the channels would no longer have a negative programming option.

That time will never come. The wise King Solomon taught us that G-d created the world in perfect balance. That we will always have a balance of good and bad in our life. That we will always have a balance between abundance and scarcity at any given time in our life.

You have the ability to make choices that will determine which side of the perfect balance in your life you choose to tend to and manifest. For example, if you take the time every day to be grateful and appreciate the many blessings you already have, you will gain the experiences that are essential for your peace and happiness.

Appreciating what you have now keeps you grounded and living in the present moment. Practicing appreciation allows you to feel that where you are right now is a wonderful place to be. You want to be able to say, "I love where I am on the way to some place better." You need to "achieve happily" and not "happily achieve" if you want to experience heaven on earth.

Researchers say that we have sixty thousand thoughts a day, most of them automatic, which means once we change a thought and choose which emotion we choose to supercharge, then those emotions will work for us even in our down times.

Since you're hardwired to be happy, positive thoughts take root and get supercharged a lot faster than their negative counterparts. The proof can be seen in babies. Unless they are experiencing digestive problems they always seem happy. They're hardwired to be happy.

So were you when you were born until a negative experience changed your programming. The goal is to revert to your original programming and roll back to the happiness you experienced as a baby.

In addition to controlling your thoughts or your focus, you also need to control your behavior, specifically what you say. Our gift of speech is extremely powerful. King Solomon, the wisest man, talks about its power: "Death and life are in the power of the tongue," he says in The Proverbs. You have the ability to choose what you will say and thereby facilitate life or death.

Let me demonstrate the power of our words and their effect on our emotions.

Suppose for a second that a close friend of yours develops leukemia and has three weeks to live. What word would you use to describe this? Perhaps the word "terrible"?

I find that most of the people I do this exercise with use a word that they have used in the past to describe any life limitation. They may even describe their anxiety as "terrible." But anxiety can be described as terrible only if it measures the same as the above example. I urge you to choose another word to describe your experience.

One additional example would be to take a visit to a mental institution. Observe an individual who is heavily medicated and crying. Now think about how you would define this in a word. How about the word "depressed"? Did the description of depression ever surface in your mind to describe yourself? Was it appropriate compared with the individual in the mental institution?

The words you choose are a result of your brain's emotional filing cabinets, which have many classifications for you to choose from whenever you need one.

It is possible for you to design a fresher and more positive file folder system in your memory bank, by choosing to give experiences a new word. This will reduce the chances of accessing a folder that evokes old, less resourceful emotions. Choose to use empowering words like "outstanding," "passion," and "amazing."

When you use the same word to describe an old experience, even in the event that you made progress to fuel your success cycle and create momentum, your brain does not recognize a difference. The results are not recognized, and the success cycle is short-circuited.

EXERCISE

If you want to understand the benefits you can derive from just this one small adjustment to your language, try the following exercise.

Make a list of the negative emotions and positive emotions you have felt in response to various situations over the past week.

Negative Emotions

1.

2.

3.

4.

5.

Positive Emotions

1.

2.

3.

4.

5.

If you're like the many people I have helped with this exercise, you will find that you have experienced more negative than positive emotions. You will also find that you're very limited in your emotional vocabulary – you have only a few emotional filing cabinets that all your experiences must fit into. When you're limited in your emotions and most of them are negative – you are setting yourself up for failure.

Here's a surprise for you: There are over six thousand words for emotions in the Webster's dictionary, so you have a huge resource to explore in learning new, positive emotions. This will widen your repertoire and, most beneficial of all, the new words you begin to use will improve the quality of your life.

Fake It Till You Make It

"Fake it till you make it" is another great management technique. If you fake being vibrant and healthy, it has the same impact on your emotional mind as a dose of antidepressant medication. Other findings have shown that depressed individuals were able to accomplish the same desired result of the synthetic drug they were prescribed by smiling in the mirror for half an hour a day instead.

Here's another way you can recognize the power of your behaviors on your emotional experience. Imagine if I told you that an individual on the other side of a door was happy and asked you the following questions: Is she smiling or frowning? Are her shoulders up or down? Is her breathing shallow or full? Is she looking up or down?

In my experience, no matter what continent or country you live in, you will answer these answers correctly.

Now, if I asked you the same set of questions, only now the person on the other side of the door was depressed, you would probably get the answers right as to what that person looked like.

Why would you be able to do that? Do you have psychic abilities? Do you have x-ray vision? Of course not. You simply know instinctively that humans manifest happiness or depression in certain ways physiologically. This applies to any other emotion as well. You can peek into a room of people and know if it's a wedding or funeral based on the way everyone's behaving.

The Ingredients of Any Emotion

The recipe for an emotion is made up of ingredients from three different categories:

- thought,

- language, and

- behavior.

Start creating a new recipe book to get into optimal emotional states. Put the right ingredients together any time you choose to be in a particular emotional state.

Mindfulness

One final skill that will enhance your quality of life is called mindfulness, a skill that is particularly helpful when an issue and an emotion become fused and you don't know how to break the connection.

Look around the room you're in. You will notice many items of various sizes – large pieces of furniture or appliances and many smaller items as well. The same is true of your emotional experience. Many emotions and problems or issues – large and small – exist in your life. However, just as a large piece of furniture in a room doesn't keep the room from being utilized successfully, so too there are many large issues in life that don't have to stymy your functionality.

Life comes with the guarantee that you will die one day, and that is a sad thought which is considered large. However, you move through your life just fine and function fully with that present in the emotional room of your mind.

Now let's take a small thought, one that's just the size of your hand. There are many of them in your room and they don't get in the way of life. Now move your hand in front of your eyes. Can you see anything? Can you continue to function this way? Of course not. Your vision is totally blocked – at best you can peek out from some corner. Your life is totally affected even though the issue is smaller than many other items in your room.

Similarly, small emotions or problems, because they're right in front of your mind's eye, can paralyze you and keep you from moving ahead with your life.

When you become fused with your problem, you need to move the problem away from your eyes to somewhere else in the room. You need to separate yourself from the problem. It will still be in your room, but now you can move ahead.

Mindfulness training helps you do just that – to separate yourself from your racing mind. Practice being a bystander on the outside looking in. Watch your mind sprint by. Or visualize yourself sitting alongside a stream, watching your thoughts and emotions flow downstream past you. The point of this type of exercise is to remain emotionally detached.

EXERCISE

Achieving a State of Mindfulness

The following exercise will help you achieve a state of mindfulness.

Begin by finding a quiet place. Sit with your head, neck, and back straight, but not stiff.

Try to put aside all thoughts of the past and the future and stay in the present.

Become aware of your breathing. Sense the air moving in and out of your body. Feel your belly rise and fall, with the air entering your nostrils and leaving your mouth. Pay attention to the way each breath changes and is different.

Watch every thought come and go, whether it is fear, anxiety, worry, or hope. When thoughts come up in your mind, don't ignore or suppress them but simply note them. Remain calm and use your breathing as an anchor to re-center yourself.

If you find yourself getting carried away in your thoughts, observe where your mind went and, without judging, simply return to your breathing. Remember not to be hard on yourself if this happens.

As the time comes to a close, sit for a minute or two, becoming aware of where you are. Open your eyes slowly and get up gradually.

Start your day with this mind exercise. After work is also a good time to go into this space, or before you take on a series of tasks. The clarity that comes from this experience will enhance the moment you're in so you can enjoy whatever you're winding down from or taking on.

When beginning this exercise, start with two minutes and eventually work up to ten minutes. This will exercise your mind and build concentration, giving you the ability to break any mental pattern and move into a different space. You can utilize this technique to move from a non-desired pattern to a more empowering one.

KEY 5

SET AND ATTAIN YOUR GOALS

SET YOUR GOALS

No personal development program worth its salt fails to discuss goals and their importance. As the saying goes, "If you don't know where you're going, any road will get you there." You can't get anywhere without knowing the address. It's true that the world's most capable computer sits between your ears, but if you don't give it clear instructions, it can't deliver.

Or, to use another analogy, the first step in building a new house is to create an idea of what the end product will look like. Then you can work the details of what you want to have in it. Based on that, you can develop the blueprint. Once you have the blueprint, you can create a plan for actually building the house.

The first step in achieving the life you deserve and desire is having a vision or a goal. You need to know what you're looking to create in your life. Goals need to be developed in every area of your life, whether financial, spiritual, relational, or personal. The clearer the goal, the better your brain can utilize its ability to shift it from idea to reality.

Don't underestimate your capability when developing your goals. You can attain any goal you wish, regardless of the fact that you do not know how to achieve it.

The universe has no limitations and has an enormous abundance for you to tap in to by using the rules that work. There are more than enough resources available for the taking. Your goals are available to you, but there are rules in the universe that you need to follow. These rules are the secret of how all the people who live the lives of their dreams have successfully accomplished their feat. Once you understand and apply them, you will own the power to create what you dream and desire and bring it to fruition.

The Difference Between Goals and Expectations

Before we work on these goals, let's look at the difference between goals and expectations. The importance of this distinction cannot be underestimated. Confusing these two concepts can be the difference between success and failure – whether you live your dream life or not.

What is the difference? It is one thing to set a goal towards achieving an outcome, which, as discussed earlier, most likely will require you to work through a fair bit of pain. It is quite another to simply *expect* an outcome, as if it will happen just because you want it to, with little work involved and certainly no pain.

A goal pulls you in the direction you choose to move towards. It is your guiding light. It gives you direction and drive so you will continue working towards your desired outcome. As you make progress and get closer to your goal, then you celebrate and fuel the success cycle. That gives you a renewed and powerful momentum, enabling you to move towards the outcome with greater precision and vigor.

Unrealistic Expectations

A positive self-image is essential for physical and psychological well-being.

If, in the course of bolstering your confidence, you set unrealistic expectations, you're setting the stage for a bout of anxiety and depression. Life is not perfect – accept it.

Exemplary performance – on the job or at home – is one way to make yourself feel good. It's commendable to work towards a goal and succeed. But what happens if you don't function up to par? You must learn to distinguish between excellence and perfection. Excellence is an acceptable goal. Allow room for growth and room for occasional error.

Consider these unrealistic expectations:

- "I should always be an amazing person…parent…spouse."
- "I should always be happy."
- "People should always treat me as I treat them."
- "I should always be more outgoing."

Be honest with yourself – these are unrealistic expectations, which are difficult, if not impossible, to achieve.

How about this scenario:

- "I expect to overcome my anxiety completely, now."

This is also not realistic. Your anxiety and depression did not appear in one second, so how can they be expected to vanish in one second?

So what happens? Your anxiety remains, and you get irritated and frustrated. You feel like a loser. You lose hope. You lose control.

How about this one?

- "I expect to see a noticeable improvement in my anxiety and depression."

This is realistic. You will feel like a winner even when you've achieved only a modicum of improvement. Your hope is reinforced, and your self-esteem is strengthened. You're motivated to continue working on recovery. You feel satisfied and content.

Set standards that reflect your values and that are within your grasp. When you reach them, you'll be thrilled and feel great; you'll be motivated to move ahead.

You need to review your expectations and adjust them realistically!

Why do you make unrealistic expectations that are destined to disillusion you? The truth is, many of your expectations are impressed on you by others. They impose their desires and expect you to deliver. You need to rework your expectations so they're realistic – so you don't fall into the throes of disappointment.

Make realistic expectations for yourself and for others. Start achieving them and enjoy the process of success!

When expectations are misunderstood and mis-utilized, the results can be detrimental. For example, if you expect to make a million dollars, earning "only" nine hundred thousand will upset you. Even though you have achieved a major success in moving towards your goal, you will be frustrated that you fell short of your expectations.

Frustration is a negative emotion that kills your drive in achieving your goals. It is the feeling of not being in control, the feeling of being out of power and being defeated. Feeling that you're not in control destroys your momentum. Your feeling of failure will hamper you from moving ahead with full force towards your goals.

Imagine that you attained 90% of your expectations. You would feel unstoppable and in control. This would empower you to have the confidence to utilize a larger portion of your personal power and supercharge yourself to get what you want.

The best thing you can do is dispose of your dysfunctional expectations, ones that you know you will probably never deliver on. Hanging on to them will only break your momentum and rob you of confidence and feelings of empowerment.

The two major perpetrators in this regard are unrealistic expectations and high expectations.

Unrealistic expectations are ones that will never happen, yet you expect them to, setting yourself up for failure. When you fail, this diminishes your momentum and self-confidence.

High expectations could happen, but they also set you up for possible failure because of how difficult they are to attain.

Don't set expectations too high. Remember, your goal is to meet your expectations 90% of the time. That will increase your momentum and build your self-confidence.

There are three categories of expectations that have great control over you:

1. Expectations you have of yourself.

2. Expectations others have of you.

3. Expectations you have of others.

These expectations must be recognized so you can successfully mitigate them and free yourself from their trap. Doing so will substantially increase the power you need to move towards your goals.

EXERCISE

Unrealistic and High Expectations

Sort out your unrealistic and high expectations, putting each one where it fits in the three categories of (1) unrealistic and high expectations you have of yourself, (2) unrealistic and high expectations others have of you, and (3) unrealistic and high expectations you have of others.

(1a) UNREALISTIC expectations you have of yourself.

1.

2.

3.

4.

5.

Ask yourself: Would I ask this of anyone else?

(1b) HIGH expectations you have of yourself.

1.

2.

3.

4.

5.

Ask yourself: Is this really my responsibility?
Who am I trying to impress? Am I trying to be perfect?

(2a) UNREALISTIC expectations others have of you (spouse, boss, society, parents, teachers, friends, others).

1.

2.

3.

4.

5.

(2b) HIGH expectations others have of you.

1.

2.

3.

4.

5.

Ask yourself: How can I be less affected?

(3a) UNREALISTIC expectations you have of others.

1.

2.

3.

4.

5.

(3b) HIGH expectations you have of others.

1.

2.

3.

4.

5.

Ask yourself: Do I really have the need to control this?

Now ask yourself how successful you would feel if you achieved 90% of your expectations. Having realistic expectations is a major key to supercharging yourself to win.

EXERCISE
Spelling Out Your Goals

Let's move ahead and begin to develop goals. Take out a pen and paper and write your goals in the following way. Imagine yourself as child in a candy store or toy store and you can have anything you desire. A child has no consideration of finances or what's realistic when picking what they want. Act the same way when you do this exercise.

Write for a few minutes without stopping. Stopping will only give you time to rationalize, and you want to avoid that as much as possible. The idea is write and dream, desire and fantasize all you can possibly want and have. Don't be realistic. Have fun with the thought that there are no limits on what your goals can be!

The following questions and areas of interest will help you create your master list of goals, hopes, wishes, and dreams. Don't limit your thinking. List everything that is exciting, even if you don't see how it could be possible. Remember that the universe can give you whatever you want.

Career Questions
If you are interested in changing careers:
Would you like to own your own business?

Would you prefer to work for someone?

What kind of work schedule would you like to have? Hours? Days?

What amount of income do you want to have?

If you like your job or profession:

What needs to change for you to have even greater job satisfaction?

What impact do you want to have?

What new skills would benefit you and your profession?

Finance Questions

How much money would you like to make annually?

How much money do you want to have when you retire?

What investment strategies do you want to have?

How much income do you want to delegate for fun and adventure?

Create a list of passive income ideas.

Personal Questions

What do you want to be, do, and have?

What emotions would you like to experience more often?

What traits would you like to adopt?

What contributions do you want to make?

What personal comforts would you like to have?

How would you like to simplify your life?

Describe your ideal day.

How much personal time would you like to have each day?

Relationship Questions

If you are looking for a new relationship:

Describe your ideal mate.

Describe the activities you will be doing.

Describe the feelings and emotions you want to experience.

If you are looking to enhance your current relationship:

What would you like to see more of?

What would you like to see less of?

Spiritual Questions

How do you want to grow spiritually?

What needs to happen for you to experience more inner peace?

How often would you like to meditate, journal, or spend time alone?

Social Questions

List the people you would like to meet. Entertainers, authors, someone you idolize.

What reputation do you want to have with family and friends?

How do you want to be remembered?

Health and Fitness Questions

What changes would you like to make to your physical body?

How often would you like to exercise each week? For how long?

What foods would you like to add to your diet?

What foods or drinks would you like to eliminate?

What chronic health problems need to be addressed?

Community Questions

What impact do you want to have on your community?

What groups or organizations would you like to join?

What special talents do you have to offer your community?

Home Questions

Would you like to have a new home? Describe it in detail.

What changes would you like to make to your present home?

What luxuries would you like to have in your home?

Learning Questions

What types of lessons would you like to take? Cooking, flying, etc.?

What books would you like to read?

What skills would you like to have or improve?

What seminars or workshops would you like to attend?

Travel Questions

Where would you like to travel?

What famous restaurants or hotels do you want to visit?

Describe your ideal vacation.

Do you want to travel first class?

Adventure Questions

List the adventures you would like to have? Climb a mountain, whitewater rafting, starring in a play?

Toys Questions

What toys or luxuries would you like to have in your life? Car, home, boat, wardrobe, electronics, computer?

What collectibles would you like to have?

Now list your goals. Keep your pen moving and just write.

1.

2.

3.

4.

5.

6.

7.

8.

9.

10.

11.

12.

13.

14.

15.

16.

17.

18.

19.

20.

21.

22.

23.

24.

25.

26.

27.

28.

29.

30.

ATTAIN YOUR GOALS

Reframing Your Goals

Now that you have named the goals you wish to attain, make sure your deepest and most valuable goals are on your list.

Now reframe them by imagining yourself at one hundred plus years, lying on your deathbed and looking back at a long life that was full of frustration and depression. Your life was empty and meaningless, and you're full of extreme regret.

An angel shows up with a message from G-d. It was decided in the heavenly courts that you will return to your current age and have the opportunity to relive your life again. What would your goals be from here on? Grab that paper and pen again and without stopping write out what those goals would be.

1.

2.

3.

4.

5.

6.

7.

8.

9.

10.

Resolving Your Conflicting Goals

The next step in the goal-attainment process is to review your goals and take note of any conflicting ones. Conflicting goals are the reason you at times may self-sabotage.

Here's an example of a conflicting goal: If one of your goals is to make a difference in your world in a way that requires interaction with people and hard work and another is to retire at forty to your own quiet island, you're in trouble. The day will come when you will get up and work really hard to build your dream goal of making a difference, and, as it is manifesting, your other goal, to retire, will kick in. At this point, your subconscious will begin to sabotage everything you have built. Your goals need to be in line with each other so you don't hamper yourself in any way from achieving them.

In most cases just recognizing your conflicting goals will free you from their grasp. Doing this requires you to decide which one is most important to you and then to move ahead to attain it.

Getting in Touch with the Why in Your Goals

They say 80% is the *why* and 20% is the *how*. In other words, if you have a big enough why, you will figure out the how. The truth is, we all know how to achieve most of our goals. Do we know how to lose weight? Of course! Eat less and become more active. Do we know how to become more fit? Get a gym membership and go every day. The "how" is quite simple. The challenge is to create a big enough why that will motivate us to actually follow through with the how.

EXERCISE

Five-Step Goal Attainment Process

Select one of your goals from the previous list and write one or two sentences about why this goal is important to you.

1.

2.

Now write one or two sentences about how you will feel when you achieve the goal.

1.

2.

Now decide on a date by which you plan to accomplish this goal.

Next, using the same goal, work through the following steps.

STEP 1

Pick one goal and write in detail why you want to achieve it and how you will feel when you do. Include as many sensory experiences as possible: tastes, sounds, smells, emotions. Use who, what, where, when, how, and why in your description. Write from the perspective that your goal has already been achieved.

Goal:

- *How did you achieve this goal?*

- *Where did help come from?*

- *What did you specifically do to accomplish this goal?*

- *Write what you are saying to yourself about your accomplishment.*

- *Write what other people are saying about your accomplished goal.*

STEP 2

Describe the kind of person who successfully achieves a goal like yours.

- *What kind of discipline is required?*

- *What attitude is needed?*

- *What belief system needs to be in place?*

- *What behaviors would that successful person have?*

STEP 3

Make a list of the resources you already have in order to accomplish this goal.

- *Who can help you? Family, friends, co-workers?*

- *What knowledge or talent do you already have?*

- *How much time do you have to devote to accomplishing this goal?*

- *How much energy do you have available?*

- *What financial resources are available?*

STEP 4

Write down what has prevented you from achieving this goal in the past.

- *List any fears, worries, doubts.*

- *Do you have any limiting beliefs?*

List any potential obstacles that could prevent you from achieving this goal now.

- *Self-sabotage?*

- *Lack of family support?*

- *Fear of success?*

- *Fear of failure?*

Now list some ideas to overcome these obstacles. Every problem has a solution.

What will you do? Challenges help you to be stronger, better, and wiser and take you to a new level of success and fulfillment.

STEP 5

Create an action plan using the information from the first four steps above. Visualize your achieved goal and work backwards to list the actions you took to achieve success.

Hint: If you want something to change, you need to work on changing your attitudes, beliefs, and behaviors now in order to see the results you want. If you keep doing what you're doing, you will keep getting what you're getting!

- *What do you need to do first?*

- *What will you do on a daily basis?*

- *What would you do differently if you had no fear around this goal?*

EXERCISE

Goal Reminder Card

Take a piece of paper the size of an index card and write down the goal from above plus three others and, in short, your reasons, your WHY, for wanting to attain these goals. Put this paper in your wallet and commit to reading it every time you use your wallet. You will be amazed at how quickly these goals will appear in your life. It is important to consistently remind yourself of these goals in order for your subconscious mind to manifest them.

KEY 6

ACCESS THE POWER OF BELIEF

TWO WAYS TO LOOK AT THINGS

Can you define the concept of belief?

Main Entry: be•lief
Function: noun

1: a state or habit of mind in which trust or confidence is
placed in some person or thing
almost always implies certitude even where there is
no evidence or proof

2: something believed; especially: a tenet or body of tenets held
by a group

3: conviction of the truth of some statement or acceptance of
some reality without direct proof

Belief is a mental state by which the mind assents to propositions, not by reason of their intrinsic evidence but because they give *you* a feeling of certainty.

The following analogy may elucidate this concept.

A belief is like a tabletop with no legs. Initially, details are provided by an outside source. You elect to regard the premise of the belief as reasonable and plausible. Once you've accepted the belief, your brain starts to reinforce it as truth – after all, you don't want to be considered a fool or liar. Each shred of evidence you provide adds another leg to your table, and your faith is intensified and fortified.

For example, consider cars. Are they good or bad?

When people who think cars are bad see an accident or a car break down, their position is reaffirmed and another leg (proof) is added to their table (belief).

In contrast, when people who think cars are good see an ambulance or emergency vehicle save a life, their position is reaffirmed and another leg (proof) is added to their table (belief).

Even when two people share the same experience, they may interpret it in vastly different ways. Two people whoosh down a ski slope. Both of them have pounding hearts and sweaty palms – evidence, for one, of the thrill of the sport, and, for the other, of a near death experience.

The following story is a brilliant illustration of this phenomenon of there being two ways to look at everything.

A man is on the way home from work after a hectic day at the office. He fights his way through the jostling crowds and finally gets on a crowded train. As luck would have it, a father and several unruly children are sitting across from him. He tries to ignore them, but they keep invading his personal space. When one of the children bumps into him, it is the last straw, and he berates the children's father for ignoring their rowdiness.

The father whispers an apology, explaining that he and his children are on their way home from a funeral – that his wife, their mother, had just been buried. He tells the man that, considering the situation, he doesn't want to rebuke them in public.

This information transforms the complainant. The circumstances do not change – the kids are still noisy and disruptive – but he quickly revises his initial belief. He is privy to new facts, which have drastically altered his impressions.

Another confusing contingency is being faced with conflicting beliefs. This puts us in a quandary. We don't know which way to turn. We stagnate – or, worse, we reach for some pleasure to numb the pain, virtually sabotaging and incapacitating ourselves.

A perfect example of this problem is weight loss.

Adolescent girls are inculcated with the idea that Woman = Thin, a belief that is endorsed by the prevalence and popularity of emaciated starlets, models, and celebrities.

Consider an adolescent girl, who, a couple of years later, is married and becomes pregnant. Suddenly she is bombarded by very different messages: You have to eat well to maintain your strength. You're eating for two. Eat so you'll have the energy to take care of your family.

Which is it? Woman = Thin or Woman = Eat? Should she diet? Should she eat?

Instead of trying to balance the two, many women lose control and alternate between binges of "pigging out" and (often unhealthy) dieting. But until this young woman decides what *she* wants, and not what everyone expects her to do, she will be pulled to and fro by this quandary.

Her challenge is to reconcile these thoughts that are at war in her mind – to adopt a lifestyle that will inspire and enlighten, to learn that it's not how you balance your diet that's important but how you balance your life.

What happens when you say to yourself: "I am a loser"? Your brain has no evidence to the contrary and accommodates the thought, proving that everything you do contributes to your failure as a productive human being. Every step you take, your subconscious will interpret as a "losing" proposition.

It is critical to adopt positive beliefs. Negativity will limit your chances of succeeding.

Still skeptical? Consider the following report.

In 1954, a young man made headlines around the world with one of the landmark events of twentieth-century sports history. At the time, it was thought to be impossible for a human being to run a mile in under four minutes. The world record of 4:01.3 had stood for nine years, and experts regarded this as an insurmountable limit.

Roger Bannister thought otherwise. He announced that

he'd run a mile in under four minutes. Everyone thought he was insane – the sports experts, the medical establishment, everyone! In 1954 he did it. Through perseverance and determination, the unbelievable became possible.

And within one year, over thirty people broke his impressive record. When asked how it was possible for so many people to run that fast so soon, Banister said, "It was never a physical boundary, only a mental one."

Prioritize and categorize your beliefs. Keep the ones that serve you, get rid of the ones that limit you, and make new ones that will get you where you want to go. Whether you can or can't do something depends on your belief in yourself. It's all up to you! You have the ability to change beliefs and change your life.

Consider this beautiful passage written by Walter D. Wintle:

If you think you are beaten, you are;
If you think you dare not, you don't.
If you want to win, but think you can't
It's almost a cinch you won't.
If you think you'll lose, you've lost,
For out of the world we find
Success begins with a fellow's will;
It's all in the state of mind…
Life's battles don't always go
To the stronger or faster man,
But soon or late the man who wins
Is the one who thinks he can.

To sum it all up: Belief is nothing more than a feeling of certainty you have about a particular idea. Belief has a major impact on your achievement of your goals and aspirations. The fact is, you see the world through your beliefs; they shape your interpretation of any event, situation, or feeling. The process is simply holding a belief, a thought you think over and over until it becomes your reality.

Belief = Behavior = Results

You may be surprised to learn that a tightrope walker, a karate master who breaks seventeen concrete slabs in a shot, an Olympic athlete, and a schoolteacher all have the same body parts, the same hours in a day, and the same access to resources. The only difference is their beliefs.

You can attain anything you want physically or spiritually if you develop the same belief system as an individual who has already attained it.

Remember my example of the two skiers coming down a ski slope? Both are panting for breath and sweating. Yet one will say that he's excited and the other that he's having a panic attack. It is their beliefs that give them totally different experiences – experiences that are based on their interpretation of what's happening.

BELIEVE LIKE THOSE WHO SUCCEED

For years studies have been published on the beliefs of successful people in order to determine how to model them. Anthony Robbins has interviewed an enormous number of millionaires and learned that they all have a very similar belief about what defines success. He has also found that the members of this group of extremely successful people share a similar belief about failure.

If you can develop the belief system of people who have already achieved greatness, you will be able to identify the quickest shortcuts to your goals. Life is too short to learn from the school of hard knocks. Model the beliefs of those who have already succeeded so you can bring all the success you desire into your own life

The best definition of success is, "I tried my best and learned something in the process." This means that even if you lost or it didn't work out, you still succeeded. Successful people recognize the virtue and significance of always fueling the success cycle. If you perceive your result as successful, then you continue the cycle and keep the momentum going.

Consider the inspirational story of Walt Disney. After approaching 303 banks to get a loan to actualize his idea, he finally succeeded. What was his belief about his 302 "failures"? To him, each one was a success, because he tried his best and learned in the process how to make his sales pitch better. This ultimately led to his getting the loan he needed to create the theme park that paid off – big time.

The same is true across the board for successful people. Another example is Colonel John Sanders, the father of Kentucky Fried Chicken. He found himself retired at age sixty-five with an old Cadillac Roadster and a $105 pension check.

He also had a great recipe for chicken. He figured he could sell his chicken recipe and get wealthy because he believed others would love it, too. The story goes that he weathered 1,008 rejections and got his first yes on prospect number 1,009, and the rest is history. By 1963, he had 600 restaurants selling chicken with his recipe. He had achieved his goal.

Today, given worldwide advances in communications, we can get the word out there fast. A Walt Disney of today could apply to 304 banks with a few clicks of a mouse. This makes the rejection process much easier. We have to endure only a little rejection and have minimal success to achieve our goals.

J. K. Rowling is another good example. In a short time, she went from being a clinically depressed single mom to selling 400 million books and becoming number 12 on the Forbes richest in the UK, worth just shy of $800 million. All she needed to endure was twelve rejections before landing her first opportunity.

You need to implement a new rule for rejection. A rejection has the power to affect you only if you agree with it 100%. Also, always remember that *you* are not being rejected, just your idea.

Massive rejection is the right track to success.

Now ask yourself, what would you do if you knew you couldn't fail? Probably anything! So go do it, because you're the one making the rules for feeling that you failed.

Successful people define failure as giving up. If you don't give up, you don't fail and are still in the game. So just like your belief about success, your belief about failure will determine whether you're the next Walt Disney, Colonel Sanders, or J. K. Rowling. You can learn to adopt new, empowering beliefs and also how to let go of limiting beliefs.

Beliefs can limit you not only emotionally but also physically. This is clearly illustrated in the example of the runner I mentioned earlier, Roger Bannister. Until 1954 it was believed that the human heart could not sustain the running of a mile in less than four minutes. That is until this determined athlete broke the record and accomplished the feat.

It turns out that he actually changed the consensus on what was possible for the human heart to achieve. His world record lasted only forty-six days. Thousand have broken his record in the years since. Because he changed athletes' beliefs, he changed what was possible for them to achieve.

CHOOSE YOUR BELIEFS CAREFULLY

Choosing your beliefs carefully can make you rich and strong and even make you live longer.

You need to choose your beliefs carefully since, ultimately, they will determine outcomes in your life.

A major area of concern is conflicting beliefs. Conflicting beliefs are a major cause of anxiety, stress, and limitation, also referred to as internal conflict.

When we have conflicting beliefs, we tend to let go of our dream instead of letting go of the belief that is limiting us.

What you believe is what is real to you. So by realizing and choosing your beliefs, you are in essence creating your world as you will experience it.

Remember that first you accept a belief, and then your brain proves it by interpreting events to coincide with the belief.

If you believe that an individual has your best interest in mind, your brain will interpret everything to keep that true for you. The opposite is also true: if you believe someone is out to hurt you, your brain will interpret everything they do as negative.

The saying "Whether you think you can and cannot, you are right" is true for this reason.

STARVE YOUR OLD BELIEFS

Irrational Beliefs

Another problem is the way we hold on to irrational beliefs. We can spend a lifetime thinking incorrectly. We need to be sure that our beliefs are rational. Find people you trust to help you sort your beliefs out, or draw on the beliefs of others who have succeeded.

Remember, you are the creator of your beliefs. When nurtured, your new beliefs will become new behaviors, and your old beliefs, because they are no longer reinforced behaviorally, will die of malnutrition.

EXERCISE
Beliefs That Will Serve You Best

Answer these questions to help you choose beliefs that will serve you best:

1. What belief can you adopt that will make you feel less stressed?

2. What belief would make you more assertive?

3. *Think of a calm person you know. What belief(s) does he/she possess that infuse him or her with a sense of poise and peace of mind?*

4. *What five beliefs are getting in the way of you achieving your goals?*

    1.

    2.

    3.

    4.

5. *What five beliefs, if developed, would get you closer to your goals?*

    1.

    2.

    3.

    4.

    5.

KEY 7

MAINTAIN YOUR POWER

MAINTAIN YOUR GAINS

To paraphrase the famous saying attributed to Albert Einstein, "If you think and act the same way you did yesterday, it is ludicrous for you to expect different results." To achieve different results, you must change your thoughts and deeds.

This book's first six keys showed you how to supercharge yourself to win. This seventh and last key is just as important, because it will help you hold your gains and continue towards your goals and aspirations.

Take a moment to understand what got you stuck in the first place, then do all you can to never go back to your old ways again.

To change is a most difficult task. If it were simple, you would have conquered your limitations a long time ago.

Why is change so difficult and complicated for us, dissuading us from divesting ourselves of our limitations?

The reality, as harsh as it may sound, is that we cling to our limitations. We may prefer to remain shrouded in profound obscurity. It's our decision. This is not to say that it represents a deliberate or conscious effort. Obviously we dislike our limitations. But consider this: We will actually set about accruing benefits – secondary gains – to make our limitations acceptable!

A common, enticing, and alluring secondary gain is avoiding change.

Change is a venture into the unknown. Change is uncomfortable. We do whatever we must to avoid that feeling. So we stay anxious and depressed.

This is a vicious cycle that must be broken. We must recognize that by doing nothing we will never escape the morass we're in. We must accept discomfort if we are to overcome our limitations.

Our penchant for self-delusion is colossal. Taking the blame for our state of mind and accepting liability are hard pills to swallow. Denial and depression are easier.

Think about it. You are a communal creature of habit and enjoy your conventional routines. Should you be so bold as to presume to change, you will compel others to recalibrate their lives as well. And you don't want to be the source of discomfort for your family, friends, and business associates.

Differentiating between pleasure and satisfaction is complicated. Both can be addictive. Both create a sense of contentment.

Pleasure is wonderful, but it is a fleeting sensation.

The consequences of satisfaction, however, are timeless.

The pleasure of taking the easy way out, staying in your rut, and not working on modifying your behavior can never compare with the satisfaction of regaining self-confidence and feeling truly alive.

Don't resist the opportunity to change. You won't regret breaking the addiction of negative and limited thinking. The consummate sense of satisfaction is incomparable. Trumping limitations will make you a happier person...a better person.

RITUALS FOR SUCCESS

One of the best ways to overcome the likelihood of relapsing into old, negative habits is to develop rituals. Rituals are the things you do every day without thinking. No power struggle is involved; you just do them naturally.

You already have rituals in the way you get dressed, eat, interact with your loved ones, and take care of your bodily needs. You probably do not struggle with these behaviors, because they require no conscious thought. In essence, they happen on their own, like scratching yourself when you have an itch.

Successful people have rituals by which they do things that empower them to achieve their goals. Just watch professional baseball players. They follow their own specific ritual before they perform. Maybe it's kicking in the sand or spitting. Their ritual helps them behave in a way that helps them win.

Their real ritual, though, is practicing; that is what got them to be one of the best players in the world. They practiced for thousands of hours and became great. During their practice, they created rituals that enabled them to perform in abundance without thinking or struggling with their mind.

The most successful salespeople I've ever met or read about have power rituals that enable them to do what they need to do without a mental struggle. Some use the ritual of making a specified number of calls within a certain time frame each day. They don't even think about it. It's just what they do, like getting dressed and brushing their teeth.

Those who are committed to regularly working out at the gym succeed in reaching their wellness goals. They have created a ritual that runs on its own with no conscious input.

EXERCISE

Develop a Power Time

Create a fifteen- to thirty-minute exercise routine daily and divide the time into three quadrants. You can do your mental exercises and physical exercises combined. There is benefit in combining them whenever possible, because the endorphins produced while exercising become anchored to your goals and speed up their coming to fruition.

Quadrant 1

In the first quadrant, focus on what you can be grateful for in your life (refer to the gratitude list you created earlier) and fully associate with it. Write it down here.

Come up with two or three answers to the questions that follow and feel the feeling. If you have difficulty discovering an answer, simply use the word "could" in the questions. Example: What could I be most happy about in my life now?

A) What am I happiest about in my life now?

What about that makes me happy? How does that make me feel?

B) What am I most excited about in my life now?

What is it about that which makes me excited? How does that make me feel?

C) What am I proudest of in my life now?

What makes me proud of that? How does that make me feel?

D) What am I most grateful for in my life now?

What makes me grateful for that? How does that make me feel?

E) What am I enjoying most in my life right now?

What about that do I enjoy? How does that make me feel?

F) What am I committed to in my life right now?

What makes me committed to that in my life? How does that make me feel?

G) Who do I love? Who loves me?

What makes me loving about that? How does that make me feel?

Quadrant 2

In the second quadrant, focus your goals in the present tense –
imagine that you already have them. Describe what it's like to
live now that you've achieved them.

Quadrant 3

In the third quadrant, affirm beliefs that you want to engrain in
your mind. Repeat them over and over.

Use the following when creating your affirmations.

Positive Phrases

- *I'm choosing to be calmer and relaxed every day.*
  (Not: I'm not going to have anxiety any more.)

Emotion-Provoking

- *Use feeling words such as easily, joyfully, effortlessly, boldly.*
- *Use words that are fun and passionate.*

Present Tense

- *The subconscious mind does not understand past or future,
  only the here and now.*
- *You must affirm your goals as if you have already attained
  them:*
  - *"I have…"*
    "I am…"
    "I always…"

Personal

- *It's okay to use general affirmations, but the more personal you can make your positive self-talk, the more quickly you will see results.*

CONCLUSION

I'm confident that you have taken tremendous strides on our journey together in this book and have made incredible progress. You understand where you are in your life at this moment and have a handle on your feelings. Most importantly, you now can access skills to help you deal with the ups and downs of life.

You will integrate limitation-buster strategies into your life according to your personal needs.

Your Steps to Success

- IDENTIFY what's getting in your way. Identify your limitations.

- RECOGNIZE the thought patterns that amplify your limitations.

- BELIEVE in your power and ability to improve your sense of self.

- ORGANIZE the tactics and techniques that will help you meet your goals

- PRACTICE! Repeat, repeat, repeat. The results will surprise you.

- PERSIST! Stay committed to yourself and you will succeed

When you follow these steps to success, you'll be amazed at the changes you will see in yourself.

Incorporate the following helpful tools in your daily routine.

- Have a power-time session every day.
- Practice diffusion and relaxation skills by living with mindfulness.
- Treat yourself the way you would treat someone you care about.
- When you attain your goals, never forget to celebrate your achievement.

Remember, you have what it takes to begin supercharging yourself to win and break through your limitations. By utilizing the seven keys that you have acquired through this book, you have the power to unlock your potential and achieve the life you desire and deserve.

Blessings for a great life!
Ben

ABOUT BENJAMIN HALPERN

As an experienced business professional and licensed clinical social worker, Benjamin is passionate about applying his skills and knowledge in personal development to help thousands create the positive life changes they desire. From his earliest days in sales management to owning a real estate development company, his business philosophy has always centered on bringing out the very best in those around him. Ben is the developer of the Staying on Track...One Step at a Time™ program for dealing with anxiety and stress and is the President of the F.A.S.T. Center for Personal Development. For more information, to schedule a consultation, or to book a speaking engagement, please call F.A.S.T. Center for Personal Development, 732-730-3900.

Lightning Source UK Ltd.
Milton Keynes UK
UKHW020739180319
339357UK00011B/516/P